easy
Lotus Notes R5

See it done

Do it yourself

que®

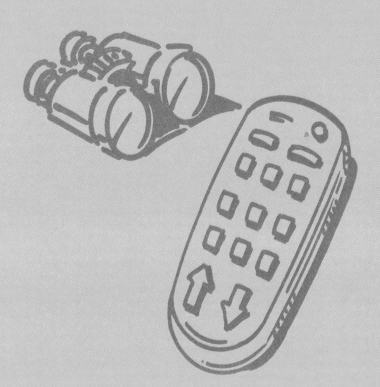

Copyright © 1999 by Que Corporation

International Standard Book Number: 0-7897-2106-6

Library of Congress Catalog Card Number: 99-62410

Printed in the United States of America

First Printing: October 1999

02 01 00   4 3 2

Trademarks

Warning and Disclaimer

About the Author

Cate McCoy is co-founder and President of AlphaPoint Systems, Inc., a computer consulting company located north of New York City. AlphaPoint specializes in custom system development including Lotus Notes Domino, Windows, and relational databases. You can visit AlphaPoint at www.alphapointsys.com, their Lotus Notes Domino Web site.

Cate divides her time between consulting, teaching, and writing. Her authoring credits include course materials for Learning Tree International, computer-based training modules, and countless systems proposals for client prospects. As a trainer, her audience has included professional software developers, undergraduates in Mount Saint Mary's computer science classes, end-users at General Motors and IBM, and her teenage children, James and Dana, who naturally know more than Mom anyway. When she manages to tear herself away from her computer, you can find Cate hanging out at the local airport getting ready to take to the sky in her Cessna 172.

Dedication

This book is dedicated to the bookends that define my life—my parents and my children.

Acknowledgments

This book is no exception to the rule that everything in life is a collaboration of forces, whether they are forces of nature, circumstance, or people. The energy contributed by my editorial and publication teams is much appreciated. The neglect suffered by my friends and family during the deadline days can never be forgiven but is definitely acknowledged…thanks for sticking by me. Finally, the heroes in my life deserve acknowledgement for always being mentors of the highest caliber in both spirit and example: Abraham Lincoln, Theodore Roosevelt, Steve Bock, and Russ Lange.

Executive Editor
Christopher A. Will

Development Editor
Kate Shoup Welsh

Managing Editor
Thomas F. Hayes

Project Editor
Leah Kirkpatrick

Copy Editor
Victoria Elzey

Proofreader
Tricia A. Sterling

Indexer
Christine Nelsen

Technical Editors
Karen Fishwick
Victor Mascari

Production
Stacey DeRome
Ayanna Lacey
Heather Miller

Illustrator
Bruce Dean

How to Use This Book

It's as Easy as 1-2-3

Each part of this book is made up of a series of short, instructional lessons, designed to help you understand basic information that you need to get the most out of your computer hardware and software.

Click: Click the left mouse button once.

Double-click: Click the left mouse button twice in rapid succession.

Right-click: Click the right mouse button once.

Pointer Arrow: Highlights an item on the screen you need to point to or focus on in the step or task.

Selection: Highlights the area onscreen discussed in the step or task.

Click & Type: Click once where indicated and begin typing to enter your text or data.

Each step is fully illustrated to show you how it looks onscreen.

Task 55: Deleting and Undeleting Files

⚠ Tips and ⚠ Warnings give you a heads-up for any extra information you may need while working through the task.

Each task includes a series of quick, easy steps designed to guide you through the procedure.

Items that you select or click in menus, dialog boxes, tabs, and windows are shown in **Bold**. Information you type is in a **special font**.

Drag

Drop

How to Drag: Point to the starting place or object. Hold down the mouse button (right or left per instructions), move the mouse to the new location, then release the button.

Next Step: If you see this symbol, it means the task you're working on continues on the next page.

End Task: Task is complete.

Easy Lotus Notes R5

Lotus Notes R5 is an exciting software program designed to make the electronic information age a little easier for you. In a world that often seems shrouded in clandestine technical maneuvers, Lotus Notes R5 shines as a unique tool that lets you create, store, and easily find information. What kinds of information? All kinds! For instance, you can use Lotus Notes to access information from electronic mail (email), your calendar, word-processing documents, the Internet, your personal computer's hard drive, and even your Palm Pilot!

Lotus Notes R5, or **Notes**, stores its information in containers called **databases**. You'll see this term used a lot throughout Notes. Don't let it scare you, however; it's just a term that means a collection of related information has been grouped together so that you can work with it easily.

Easy Lotus Notes R5 gets you going quickly with clear, step-by-step, visual instructions on how to use the Notes client to manage electronic information. From starting Notes to exiting Notes to everything in between, you'll get no-nonsense information on how to complete tasks that make your life easier in this age of information.

Get Started with the Lotus Notes R5 Client

Early in 1999, Lotus introduced Lotus Notes R5 as a major upgrade to the previous R4 version of the product. Many of the differences between R5 and R4 are easily visible. For example, what you see on the screen in R5 is completely different from what you see in R4.

This section covers the basics of starting, working with, and exiting Lotus Notes R5. The step-by-step instructions show you how to use R5 in Windows NT; however, the steps are the same in Windows 95 and Windows 98. Other operating systems, such as OS/2, are similar. When you're done with this section, you'll be comfortable moving around by using windows, menus, and icons in the Lotus Notes R5 client.

Tasks

Task 1: Starting Lotus Notes R5

You're a few clicks away from a very satisfying software experience, so away we go! Starting Lotus Notes R5 from Windows NT is done directly from the desktop like most programs that run on a Windows platform.

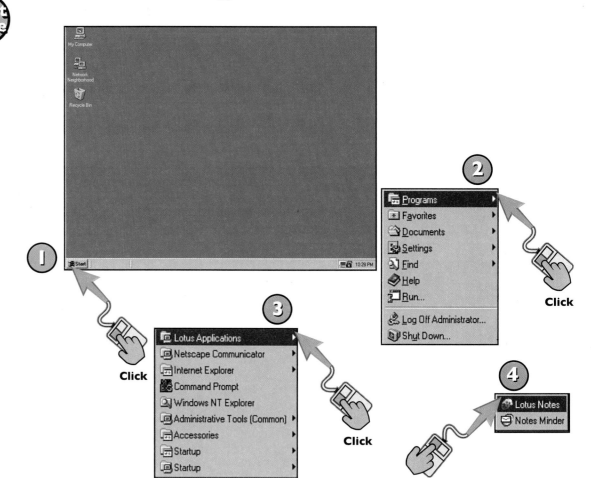

✓ **Lotus Notes Shortcut**
If a Lotus Notes R5 shortcut icon is visible on your Windows desktop, you can double-click it to start Lotus Notes.

✓ **Non-Windows Software**
If you're using Lotus Notes R5 on a UNIX, Macintosh, OS/2, or mainframe client, follow the standard procedures for starting programs on that platform.

① Click the **Start** button on the Windows taskbar.

② Choose **Programs** on the Start menu.

③ Choose **Lotus Applications** from the list of programs.

④ Choose **Lotus Notes** to start the R5 client.

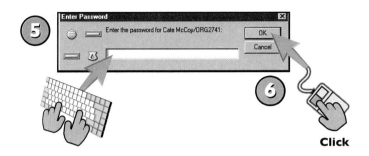

Click

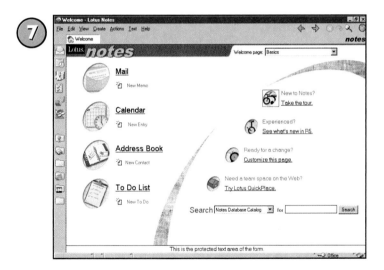

5 Type your Lotus Notes password.

6 Click the **OK** button.

7 The Lotus Notes R5 Welcome page is displayed.

✓ **Passwords**
Lotus Notes passwords are case sensitive, so make sure the Caps Lock and Num Lock features are set correctly.

⚠ **Warning**
Your Lotus Notes password may not be the same as your Windows NT (or 95 or 98) password.

Task 2: Modifying the Welcome Page

Start Here

The Welcome page is a direct path to the tasks you'll use every day. There are four built-in Welcome page styles that you can choose.

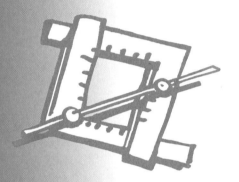

Click

Click

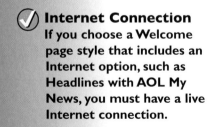

✓ **Internet Connection**
If you choose a Welcome page style that includes an Internet option, such as Headlines with AOL My News, you must have a live Internet connection.

① Click the **Welcome page** drop-down arrow.

② Click **Basics Plus**.

③ The Basics Plus page becomes your new Welcome page.

End Task

Task 3: Moving Through the Client with Bookmarks

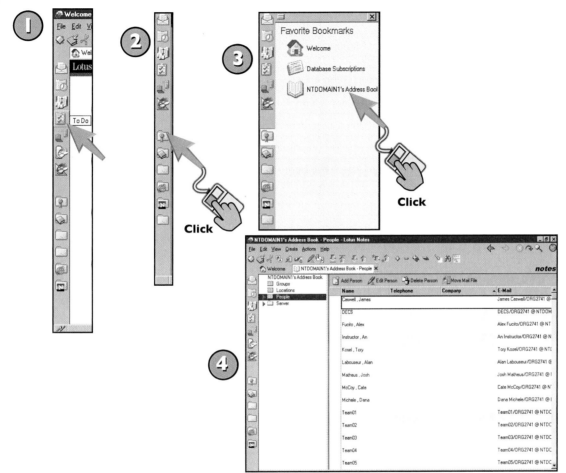

Click

Click

The vertical left border of the Lotus Notes R5 client contains *bookmarks*. Bookmarks use icons to jump you quickly between locations in Notes. Selecting a bookmark jumps you directly to another location, such as your mail file, or opens a sliding panel that contains a list of links for that bookmark. In general, the bookmarks on the top half of the bookmark list jump you directly to another location.

Pin in Place
The button at the top left of the sliding Bookmark panel can be used to create new folders and to pin the Bookmark panel in place, leaving it open.

R4 Workspace
If you've previously used Lotus Notes R4, try clicking the **Workspace** icon in the Databases bookmark to open the old-style user interface.

① Float your mouse down the left border over the icons, and read each of the bookmark labels.

② Click one of the bookmarks on the lower half of the bookmark list to view the panel containing that bookmark's links.

③ Click one of the links in the open bookmark panel, such as **NTDOMAIN1's Address Book**.

④ NTDOMAINI's Address Book appears.

Task 4: Customizing Your Welcome Page

Start Here

If one of the built-in Welcome pages isn't quite right for you, customize it by creating a new page style that includes only the options you need. When you create a new style, give it a name to uniquely identify it.

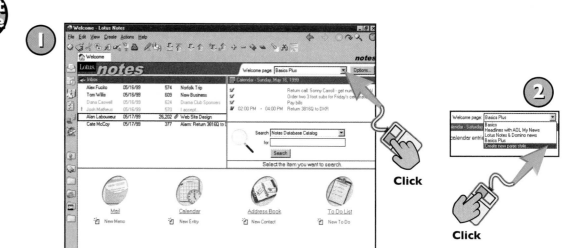

Click

Click

✓ **Page Titles**
You can create several custom Welcome pages by typing a unique and descriptive name for each one.

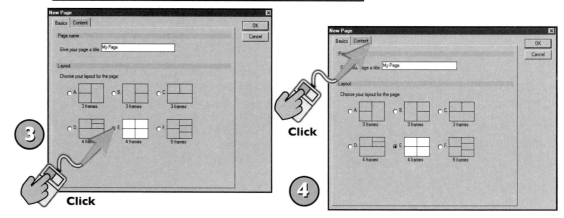

Click

Click

✓ **Deleting a Page Style**
The Options button next to the list of page styles opens the Page Options dialog box that lets you delete the selected style from the list.

① Click the **Welcome page** drop-down arrow.

② Click **Create new page style**.

③ Click one of the option buttons to choose a layout for your Welcome page.

④ Click the **Content** tab.

Next Step

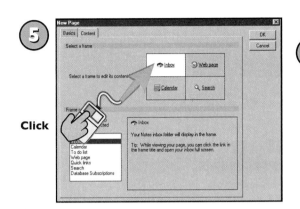

Click

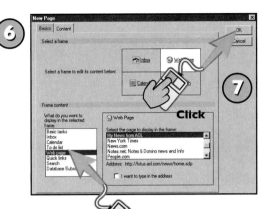

Click

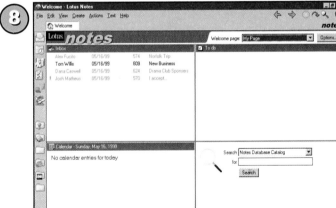

Click

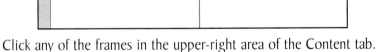

⑤ Click any of the frames in the upper-right area of the Content tab.

⑥ Click an entry in the **Frame content** list to place that item in the frame you selected. For example, to display a Web page in the selected frame, click **Web page**.

⑦ After you've made all the changes you want, click the **OK** button to save your personal Welcome page.

⑧ With your changes saved, your personal Welcome page is displayed.

Frames
Welcome page styles use a special feature called *frames*. Frames are resizable borders around areas on a screen. When you customize the Welcome page, you get to choose the content that fills the framed areas.

Task 5: Working with Multiple Windows

You can work in multiple database applications at the same time within Lotus Notes. For instance, you might have your mail Inbox open as well as your calendar. Switching between open applications is done using window tabs.

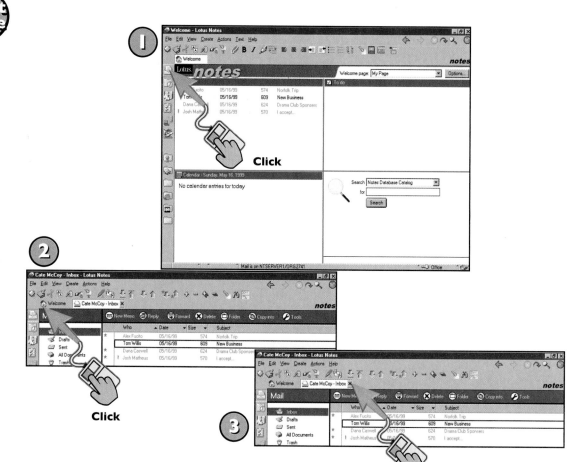

Start Here

Click

Click

Click

✓ **Which One Is the Current Window?**
Clicking the tab makes it the current window, shading the background of the tab white. The Close (**X**) button for the current window is always visible.

✓ **Cycling Through Open Windows**
Pressing **Ctrl+Tab** on the keyboard cycles you through all open windows, one at a time.

✓ **Closing a Window**
To close a window without switching to it, float the mouse over the window tab to display its **Close (X)** button, and then click it.

① Click a bookmark that opens a database, such as the **Mail** bookmark.

② The Mail window opens. Click the **Welcome** tab to switch to the Welcome page; return to the Mail window by clicking the **Mail** tab.

③ To close a window, click the **Close (X)** button on that window's tab.

End Task

Task 6: Using the Navigation Buttons

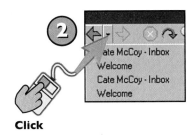

Click

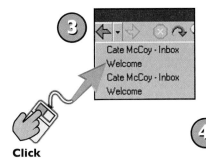

Click

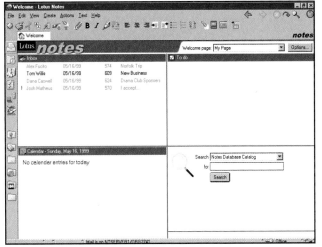

At the top-right corner of every Notes screen, universal navigation buttons provide quick access to popular tasks such as moving one page forward or backward and opening a text field where you can enter a URL to open a Web page. Some of the buttons also keep a history list that you can use to jump directly to a place you've visited previously.

1. Float your mouse over the universal navigation buttons to read their tool tips.

2. Click the drop-down arrow next to the Go Back button (clicking the **Go Back** button takes you back one page) to display that button's history.

3. Choose one of the back history pages from the list to jump directly to it.

4. You're returned to the page you selected from the history list.

 Open a URL
The Open URL navigation button opens a text area for you to type in a URL. The text area can be pinned in place so that it always appears near the top of the screen.

Task 7: Adding Standard SmartIcons to the Interface

Getting things done quickly is a major theme in Lotus Notes R5. The menu bar organizes standard Notes commands for easy use, but it's easier to use SmartIcons, which are buttons you can display to perform Notes commands quickly, often with one click instead of several menu levels. To use SmartIcons, you must first configure your interface to display them.

✓ **Positioning SmartIcons**

Use the **Position** drop-down arrow to choose a location for the SmartIcon bar. It can be displayed on the top, left, right, or bottom of the screen.

✓ **Canceling a Menu Selection**

To close a menu without making a selection, press the **Esc** button on your keyboard or click anywhere outside the menu.

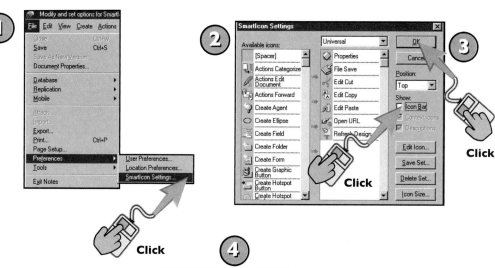

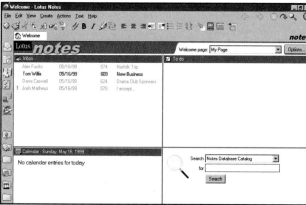

Click

Choose **File**, **Preferences**, **SmartIcon Settings....**

Click the **Icon Bar** check box to display the standard set of SmartIcons available for the current window.

Click **OK** to save the setting and display the SmartIcons.

The SmartIcon buttons are displayed below the menu.

Task 8: Customizing Your Own Set of SmartIcons

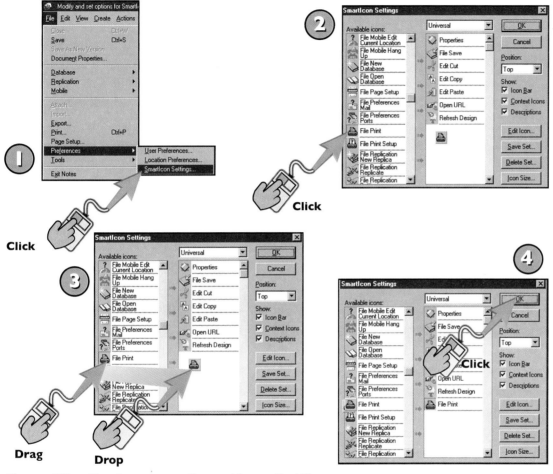

Click

Click

Drag **Drop**

The default set of SmartIcons, the universal set, contains buttons for frequently performed tasks. The available buttons change based on the context of what you are doing—for instance, editing or reading. You can also customize the set of SmartIcons to include your favorite ones all the time.

Click

✅ **Scrolling**
Scrolling can be done by holding the mouse down over the square button in the scrollbar, and then dragging up or down and releasing the mouse. You can also click in the scrolling area to move up or down a few items at a time.

✅ **Icon Size**
You can change the size of the icon from small to large (or vice versa) using the **Icon size** button.

1 Choose **File**, **Preferences**, **SmartIcon Settings…**.

2 Scroll down the list on the left and locate the task of your choice from the list of available icons.

3 Press the left-mouse button down and hold it over the task, then drag it from the list of available icons on the left to the list of active SmartIcons on the right.

4 Click the **OK** button to save your SmartIcon changes.

Task 9: Activating Keyboard Shortcuts

If your favorite way of communicating with your computer is your keyboard, you're in luck. All menu commands and many other tasks can be accessed with keyboard accelerator shortcuts.

✓ Menu Shortcuts

Any menu command with a letter underlined can be activated with the accelerator key, **Alt**, held down at the same time as the underlined letter in the menu command.

✓ Multiple Menu Commands

In a sequence of menu commands, the first action is activated using the **Alt** key held down at the same time as the underlined shortcut key. Subsequent commands in the sequence activate with the underlined key by itself. For example, to simulate opening the **File** menu and choosing **Open**, press **Alt+F** then the **O** key by itself.

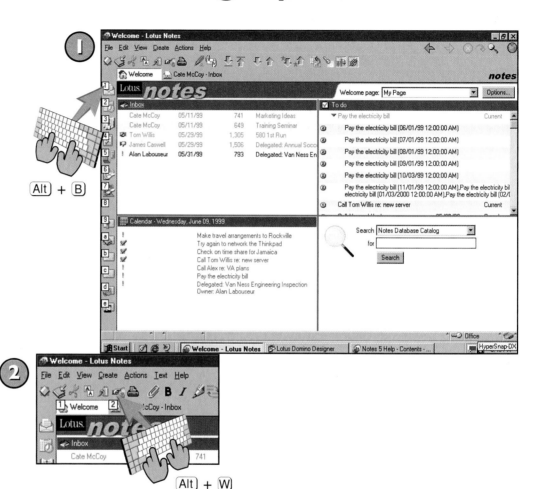

Start Here

Alt + B

Alt + W

1. Press **Alt+B** on your keyboard to display keyboard shortcuts for bookmarks; press the number **1** to open Mail.

2. Press **Alt+W** to display the accelerator keys for the Window tabs; press the number **2** to switch back to the Welcome page.

End Task

Task 10: Invoking Context-Sensitive Help

 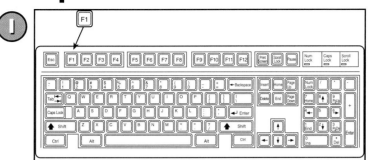

When you're in the middle of a task, you can access context-sensitive help for the task at hand. Help information is presented in its own freestanding window that you can move, minimize, and close when you're done.

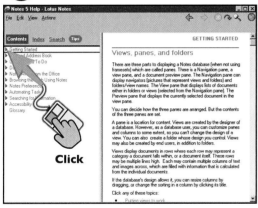

Click

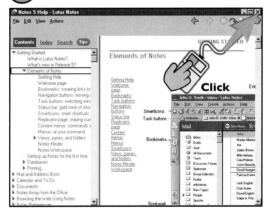

Click

✓ **Twisties**
The triangle to the left of expandable categories is known as a *twistie*. Honest! You can twist a category open or closed...expanding it or collapsing it...by clicking on the triangle.

✓ **Navigator Pane and View Pane**
The categories and topics appear on the left side of the Help screen, which is known as the Navigation pane. Detailed content information displays on the right side of the screen, which is known as the View pane.

① Press the **F1** key to open context-sensitive help.

② Click the right-pointing triangle next to any category to show its contents.

③ Click the **Close (X)** button to leave the help window.

Microsoft Windows allows you to work with multiple applications at the same time. For example, you can have Lotus Notes open at the same time as Netscape or Internet Explorer. To make working with multiple software programs at the same time easier, you can minimize Notes to the Windows taskbar, shrink it to a smaller window size, or work with it in full-screen mode.

✓ **Windows Taskbar**
The Windows taskbar is located at the bottom of the screen. The Start button is located in the left corner. Whenever an application is opened, a rectangle button for the application is added to the taskbar.

✓ **Multitasking in Windows**
Switch between open Windows applications by clicking the appropriate taskbar buttons.

Task 11: Resizing the Lotus Notes Window

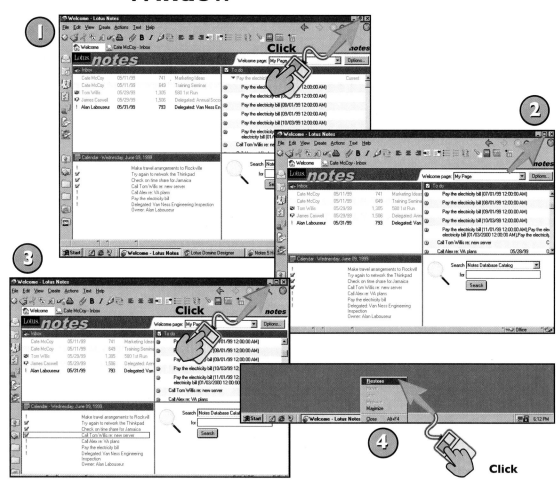

Click the **Restore** button to make the Notes window smaller than full screen. You can also resize the window by dragging and dropping its borders.

The Restore button is replaced by the Maximize button on the title bar.

Click the **Minimize** button to move Notes from the Windows desktop to the Windows taskbar.

Right-click the **Lotus Notes** icon in the taskbar and choose the **Restore** option to re-open Notes on the Windows desktop.

Task 12: Exiting Lotus Notes

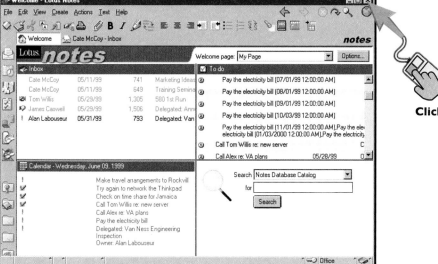

Click

Closing Lotus Notes R5 at the end of the day is a snap. Like other Windows applications, you can use the standard **Close (X)** button or the **File** menu.

Click the **Close (X)** button on the title bar to exit the Lotus Notes R5 client.

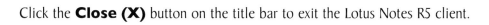 **Protecting Against Data Loss**
If you're in the middle of editing information when you decide to exit Lotus Notes, you'll be asked if you want to save the information first.

Exit Using the Menu or Keyboard
Choosing **File, Exit Notes** (or using the associated accelerator shortcut keys) also closes Notes.

PART 2

Processing Your Email

Managing your daily information needs includes keeping up with the electronic mail that passes in and out of your computer. For this task, you need easy-to-use, powerful software. Lotus Notes R5 provides all the basic mail-processing features you need plus enhanced features to help make processing your email fun.

Tasks

Task 1: Receiving Your Mail

Electronic mail delivered to you in Lotus Notes is placed in your Inbox. From there, you can do all your processing tasks.

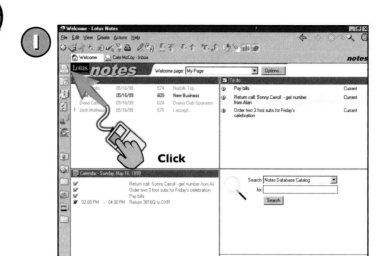

Click

Welcome Page
If your Inbox is displayed as part of the Welcome page, click the **Inbox** icon to open the mail file database.

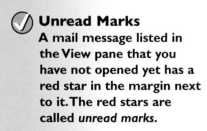

Unread Marks
A mail message listed in the View pane that you have not opened yet has a red star in the margin next to it. The red stars are called *unread marks*.

From the Welcome page, click the **Mail** bookmark to open the mail file database.

The Inbox is automatically selected for you in the Navigator pane.

The list of messages in your Inbox displays in the View pane.

Task 2: Opening and Closing Inbox Messages

Start Here

Double-Click

You read an Inbox message by opening it. This displays the contents of the message in full-screen mode. When you're done reading a message, close it to return to the list of messages in your Inbox.

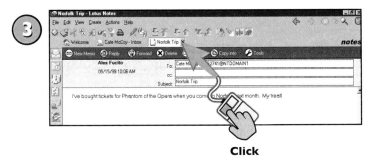

Click

(1) Double-click anywhere on the summary text of an individual message in the View pane.

(2) The message is displayed, with the address area at the top of the screen and the body of message text at the bottom of the screen.

(3) After reading a message, click the **Close (X)** button on the window tab.

Marking a Message As Read
Notes automatically marks an email message as having been read when you display it in the View pane.

Window Tabs
Opening your Inbox creates a new window with its own window tab for the mail file. Opening a message to read it creates another window with its own window tab for the message. You can quickly move between them by clicking the tabs.

End Task

Task 3: Replying to a Mail Message

When you're reading an email you received, one of the ways you can process it is to write a quick email back to the sender. Clicking the **Reply** button creates a new message from you, and automatically addresses it to the sender of the email you received.

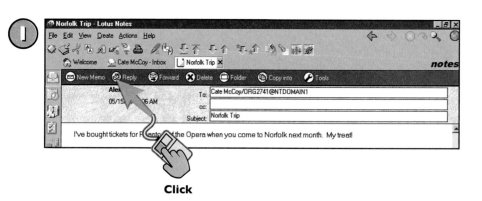

Click

✓ **Reply Options**

The Reply button has four drop-down choices that let you reply to the sender, reply and attach the original memo, reply to everyone on the To and Cc lists, and reply to everyone and attach the original memo.

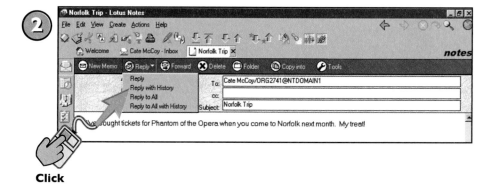

Click

✓ **Automatic Subject**

The new memo automatically fills in the subject of the message to which you're replying with the prefix *RE:*, which is a business abbreviation for *regarding*. Type over this subject if you want to change it.

① After you read the text of a message you received, click the **Reply** button at the top of the memo.

② Choose **Reply with History** to send a memo back to the sender that includes the original message.

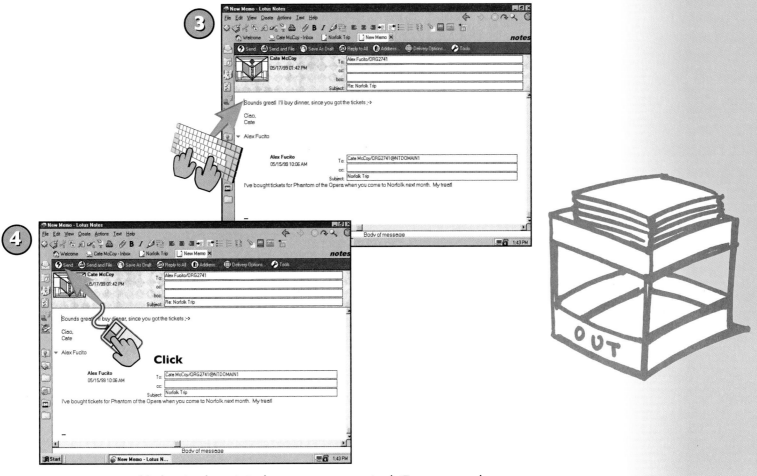

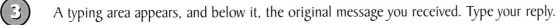

3 A typing area appears, and below it, the original message you received. Type your reply.

4 Click the **Send** button to mail the memo.

Task 4: Handling Mail Attachments

Attachments are files, such as spreadsheets, graphics, and sound files, that can appear at the bottom of an incoming email as an icon. You can open the attachment and see its contents right from within Notes.

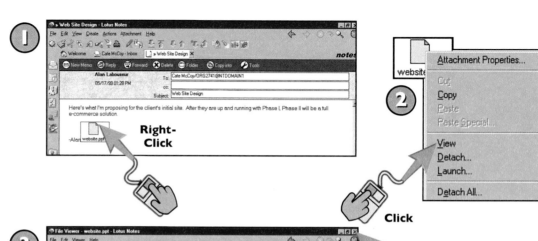

Right-Click

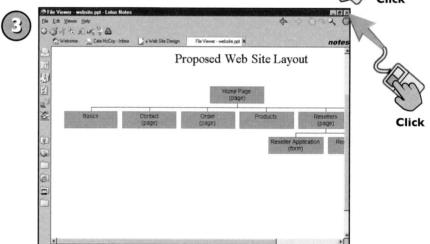

Click

Click

✓ **Attachment Indicator**
Before opening an email in the Inbox, you can tell whether it has an attached file. You'll see a paper clip at the beginning of the subject text.

✓ **Launching an Attachment**
Choosing **Attachment, Launch** opens the software that created the file, if it's available. For instance, if the attachment is a Microsoft PowerPoint file, Notes starts the PowerPoint software and displays the attachment in it.

① After reading an email that contains an attachment, right-click the icon for the attachment.

② Select **View** to display the contents of the attachment.

③ The contents of the attachment opens in Notes. Click the **Close (X)** button on the window tab to exit from the open attachment.

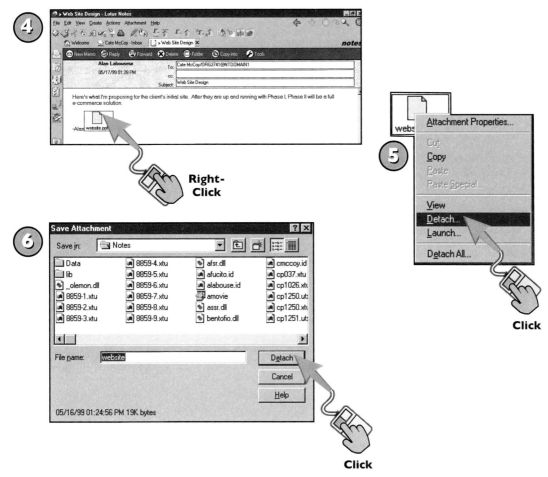

Attachment Filenames
The **Attachment** dialog box defaults to save an attachment with the same filename as the attachment. You can type a different name.

Detaching to a Specific Location
Detached attachments are saved to the current directory. You can change the location by using the **Save in** drop-down list in the **Save Attachment** dialog box.

Canceling a Detachment
Clicking the **Cancel** button in the **Save Attachment** dialog box stops the detach process before the file is saved to disk. The attachment remains in the email.

④ Again, right-click the attachment icon.

⑤ Select the **Detach...** option.

⑥ Click the **Detach** button to save the file to your PC's hard drive. The attachment file is saved to disk; in addition, it is left in the email in the mail file.

Task 5: Printing an Email

You can print the contents of an email message when you're reading the message or directly from the Inbox. Printing from the Inbox has the advantage of letting you print more than one message at a time.

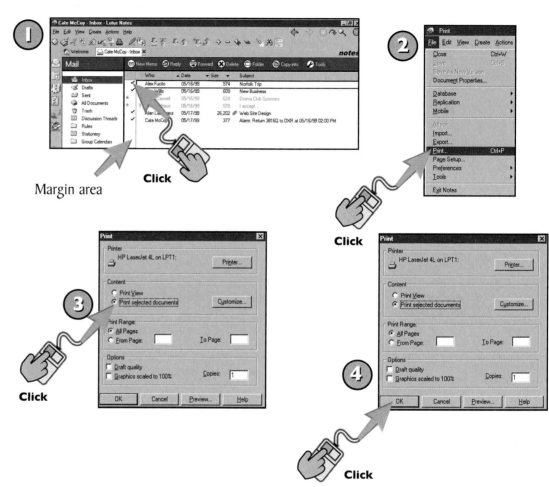

Margin area

Click

Click

Click

Click

✓ **Deselecting a Document**
To remove a check mark from a selected document, click the check mark to turn it off. Click again to turn it back on.

✓ **Printing a View**
Selecting the **Print View** option button sends the onscreen information shown in the view to the printer, resulting in a list of documents instead of the contents of a document.

✓ **Preview**
Click the **Preview** button in the Print dialog box to see an onscreen draft of what will print.

(1) Click in the margin of the Inbox View pane next to several email messages, marking each one with a check mark.

(2) Choose **File**, **Print...**.

(3) Choose the **Print selected documents** option button.

(4) Click **OK** to send the checked message to the default printer.

Task 6: Deleting Mail Messages

Start Here

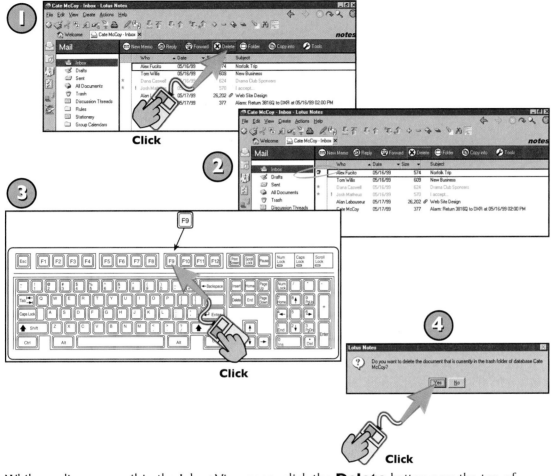

Click

Click

Click

One of the best ways to handle your mail is to read it and then delete it! Deleting is a two-step process. First, you mark it to be deleted, and then you throw it away. This gives you a chance to retrieve it before it actually gets deleted.

✓ **Deleting Multiple Documents**
Delete multiple documents from the Inbox view by selecting them (which adds a check mark) and then using the **Delete** button or key. A trash can icon appears next to each document you've deleted.

✓ **Changing Your Mind!**
If you decide not to delete a document at all and want to get rid of the trash icon next to a document, click the **Delete** button or key again. It works like a light switch; turn it on to add the trash can, or turn it off to remove the trash can.

1. While reading an email in the Inbox View pane, click the **Delete** button near the top of the screen.

2. A trash icon appears in the View margin, marking the document for deletion.

3. Press the **F9** key on the keyboard to throw the marked document out.

4. Click **Yes** when the warning message appears to permanently delete the document, or click **No** to keep the document.

End Task

Task 7: Using Mail System Folders

The Inbox is an example of a system folder; its purpose is to hold incoming messages. The Trash folder is a system folder that holds email documents that have been marked for deletion but have not yet been thrown away.

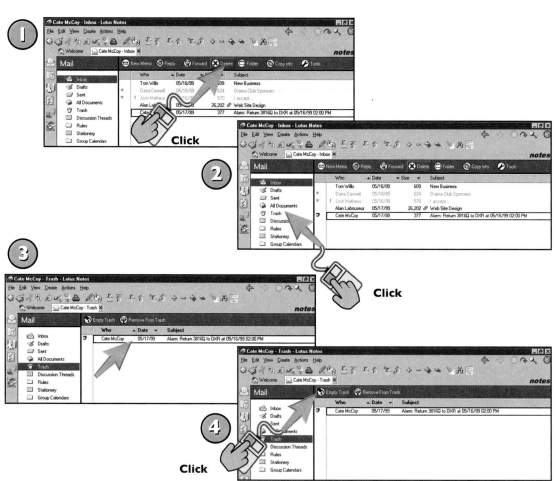

✓ **Message Mirroring**
An email message marked for deletion shows up in two places: the Trash folder and the folder you deleted it from. The Trash folder is like a mirror. It shows you all documents marked for deletion by mirroring the message from its original folder.

✓ **Emptying the Trash from the Menu**
You can empty the Trash folder by choosing **Action, Empty Trash** or the associated keyboard shortcut keys.

From the Inbox, click the **Delete** button to mark the selected message for deletion.

Click the **Trash** system folder.

The message that was marked for deletion appears in the Trash folder.

Click the **Empty Trash** button (or press the **F9** key) to throw away the documents marked for deletion.

Click

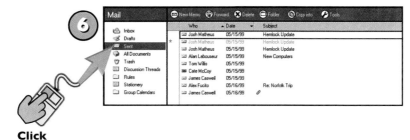

Click

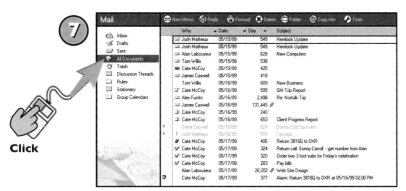

Click

5 Click the **Drafts** system folder, which contains emails that you started to write, saved temporarily, and intend to send later.

6 Click the **Sent** system folder, which contains email documents that you have already sent to other people.

7 Click the **All Documents** system folder, which mirrors all the messages in the other folders.

Task 8: Creating, Opening, and Deleting Your Own Folders

You can create your own folders in the mail file that appears below the system folders. The contents of the folders are mirrored from their original folder, so there is still only one email document.

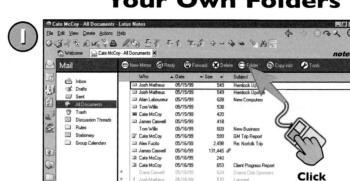

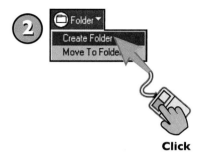

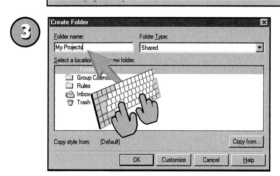

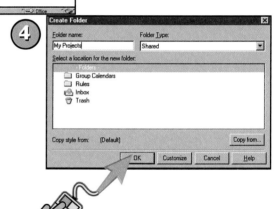

✓ Shared Versus Private Folders

Folders you create try to make themselves shared by default. *Shared* means anyone who has access to the database can use the folder. You can change the folder type to private, so only you can see and use the folder.

✓ Can't Create a Folder?

You may not be able to create shared or personal folders in a database. This is a privilege the system administrator controls.

1 Click the **Folder** button on the button bar.

2 Click the **Create Folder** option.

3 Type a descriptive name for the folder, like **My Projects**, replacing the highlighted phrase Untitled.

4 Click the **OK** button to create the new folder.

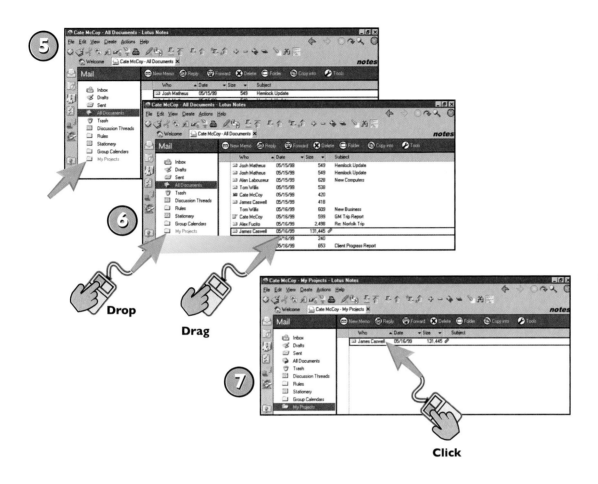

Drop

Drag

Click

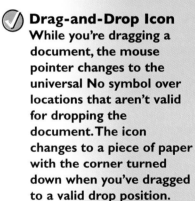

✓ **Drag-and-Drop Icon**
While you're dragging a document, the mouse pointer changes to the universal **No** symbol over locations that aren't valid for dropping the document. The icon changes to a piece of paper with the corner turned down when you've dragged to a valid drop position.

✓ **Deleting a Folder**
To delete a folder, select it, and then choose **Actions, Folder Options,** and **Delete Folder.** This deletes the mirrored copy, leaving the original document in its original location.

(5) The new folder appears below the system folders.

(6) Select a memo from another folder, press and hold the left mouse button to drag the document over top of the new folder, and release to drop the document into it.

(7) Click the new folder to see its contents.

End Task

Page
31

You can create folders within other folders, which are called *nested folders*. This is handy for organizing projects and grouping project-related email into categories.

Task 9: Organizing Mail with Folders

Start Here

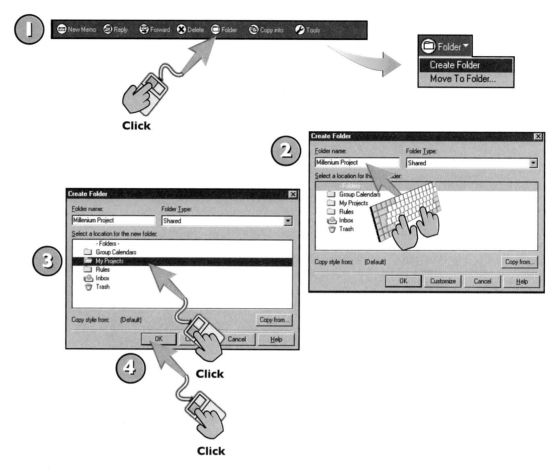

Click

Click

Click

✓ **Folder Twisties**
Nested folders display with a twistie to let you expand and collapse the folders in the group.

(1) Click the **Folder** button on the button bar, and choose the **Create Folder** option.

(2) Type a unique name for the new folder.

(3) Click one of the folders you previously created in the scrollable list of locations for the new folder.

(4) Click the **OK** button.

End Task

Task 10: Removing Messages from Folders

Start Here

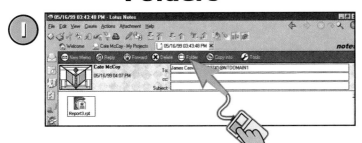

Click

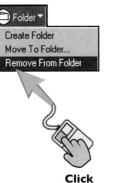

Click

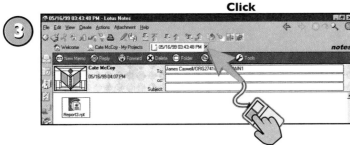

Click

Because dragging documents into your folders creates a mirrored copy of the original, deleting a document deletes it from the original location because it is the same document. To take documents out of folders you create but not delete those documents, use the **Remove from Folder** option instead of the **Delete** button.

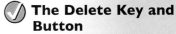 **The Delete Key and Button**
Using the Delete key on the keyboard or the onscreen Delete button in a document in one of your folders marks it for deletion and adds it to the Trash folder.

1. Double-click a document in one of your folders to open it, and then click the **Folder** button.

2. Click the **Remove From Folder** option.

3. Close the message using the **Close (X)** button.

4. The message disappears from the folder.

End Task

Task 11: Creating, Addressing, and Sending a Memo

The **New Memo button** on the button bar is the quickest way to create an email message in the Mail file database. Notes requires valid addresses for any addressees, courtesy copy recipients, and blind courtesy copy recipients.

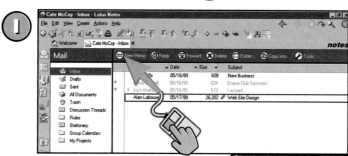

Click

✓ **Use the Address Button!**

Just like with writing and addressing an old-fashioned letter, the correct address is a necessity to guarantee that your memo will be delivered. Clicking the **Address** button is a sure way to get the address right.

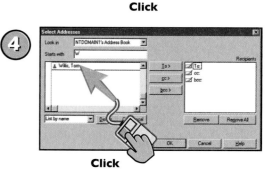

Click

✓ **Complete and Correct Addresses**

When you use the **Address** button to fill in the address fields, Notes fills in the fields with a complete and valid Notes address. After it does this, you should not type over or change the address in the memo.

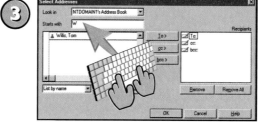

Click

Click the **New Memo** button.

Inside the new memo, click the **Address** button.

In the **Starts with** area, type the first initial of the recipient's last name to jump to that part of the address list.

Click the name in the list on the left to select it.

Next Step

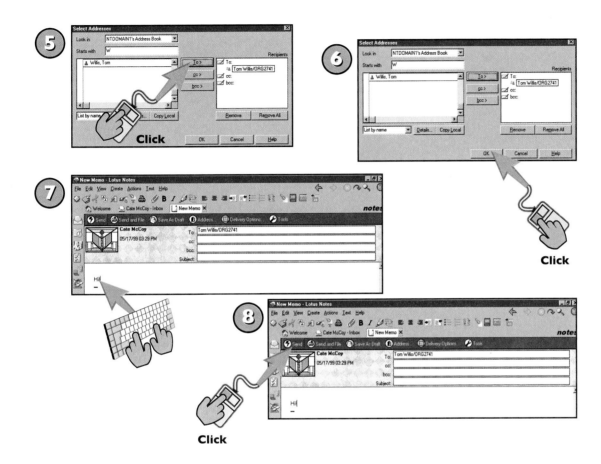

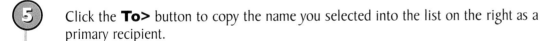

Click

Click

Click

✓ **Removing Recipients**
While you're using the Select Addresses dialog box, you can remove one or all of the recipients. To do this, select the name in the **Recipients** window and then click the **Remove** or **Remove All** buttons.

✓ **CC and BCC**
To create courtesy copy and blind courtesy copy recipients, select the name in the list on the left and click the **cc>** or **bcc>** button to add to the **Recipients** list.

✓ **Send and File**
The **Send and File** button saves a mirror copy of the memo in one of your own folders automatically.

(5) Click the **To>** button to copy the name you selected into the list on the right as a primary recipient.

(6) Click **OK** to close the Select Addresses dialog box.

(7) Click the mouse in the body typing area and type as much as you want.

(8) Click the **Send** button to send the email on its way.

End Task

Task 12: Choosing Letterhead Preferences

You can add a built-in graphic letterhead image to the top of mail that you create. This is like going to the stationery store and purchasing preprinted letterhead with a pretty picture at the top. All the memos you create include your current letterhead.

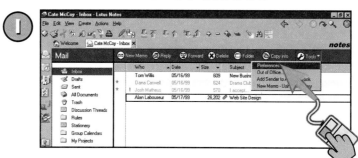

Click

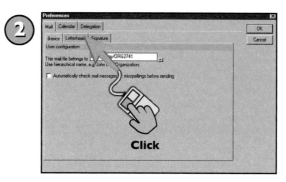

Click

✓ **Non-Notes Email Recipients**
If you're sending an email with letterhead to someone who is not using Lotus Notes as their mail system, the letterhead image is converted to a graphic attached to the memo. In this case, use the Plain Text letterhead style.

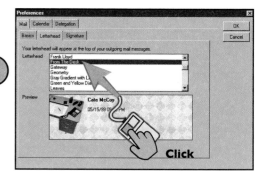

Click

✓ **Available Graphics**
Notes includes a standard, built-in set of graphic images that can be used as letterhead. Your Domino System Administrator may customize the standard set of letterhead.

1 With the Inbox displayed, click the **Tools** button on the button bar, and then click **Preferences**.

2 Click the **Letterhead** tab.

3 Select a different letterhead from the list, and click **OK** to save your change.

Task 13: Adding Your Own Attachment to a Memo

Start Here

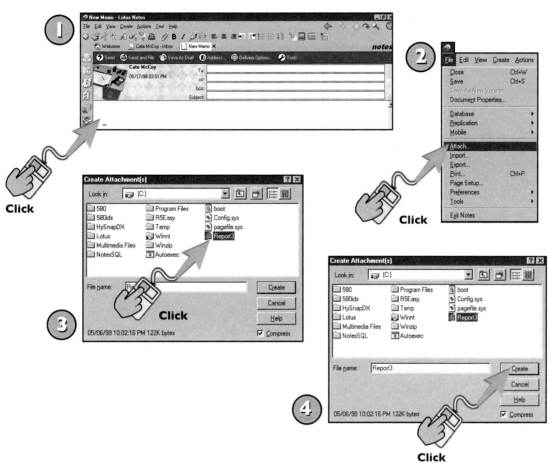

Click

Click

Click

Click

Do you need to get that **Microsoft Excel spreadsheet** or **Crystal Report** to your boss? You can do it by attaching it as a file to your outgoing email.

Attachments with a SmartIcon
Click the **Paper Clip** SmartIcon instead of opening the **File** menu and choosing **Attach**.

Compressing Attachments
The **Compress** option is automatically selected for attachments. This makes the attachment smaller for faster transmission.

1 In a memo you're creating, click in the body typing area.

2 Choose **File**, **Attach...**.

3 Use the **Look in** drop-down arrow to navigate to the location of the file you want to attach, and then click it to select it.

4 Click the **Create** button to attach the file to the email.

End Task

Task 14: Setting Delivery Options

While you're writing an email, you can change the Delivery Options to add a return receipt, automatically check the spelling, and more.

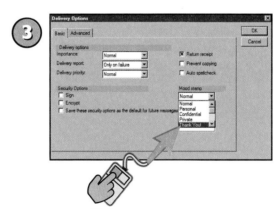

Click

Click

Click

✅ **Return Receipts**
Return receipts work only for email sent to people using Lotus Notes for email. Internet mail cannot process a return receipt.

✅ **Changing the Importance**
Setting the importance to **High** adds an exclamation mark icon to the memo when it displays in the recipient's Notes' Inbox.

① In a memo you're writing, click the **Delivery Options** button.

② Click the **Return receipt** check box to activate it.

③ Click the **Mood stamp** drop-down arrow and select **Thank You!** from the list to add a graphic to the top of the memo. Click the **OK** button to save the options.

Task 15: Saving a Memo As a Draft

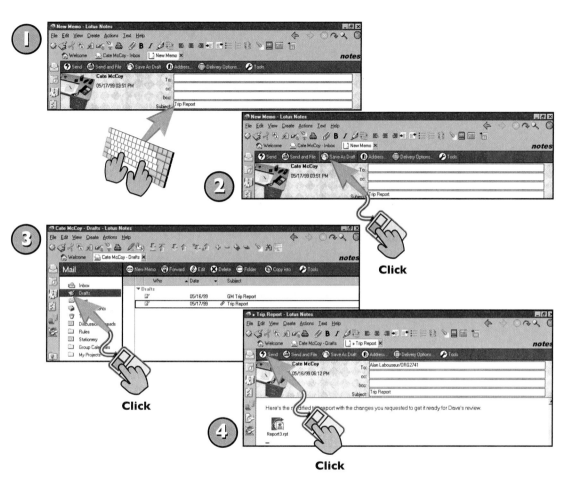

Create a draft memo when you want to save your work but not send it.

Click

Click

Click

---

1. When you're writing a memo, type a subject line.

2. Click the **Save As Draft** button.

3. Click the **Drafts** system folder to see unsent memos.

4. Open the memo, address it, and send it.

✓ **Minimum Information**
You can create a draft memo without addressing it or giving it a subject line.

Task 16: Adding Signatures to the End of Your Email

You can automatically add a text phrase, bitmap, or HTML file to the current email or every email you create using signature preferences.

Start Here

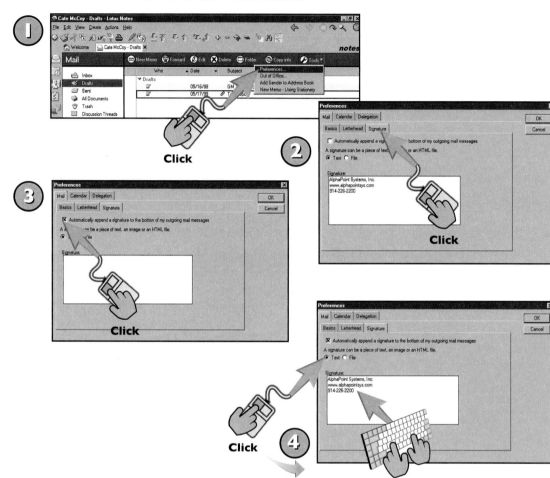

✓ **Text Signatures**
Adding your company name, Web address, or phone number are great ideas for text signatures in Notes.

1 From the Inbox, click the **Tools** button on the button bar and select the **Preferences...** option.

2 Click the **Signature** tab.

3 Click the **Automatically append a signature to the bottom of my outgoing mail messages** check box to append the signature to every email message you send.

4 For a text phrase, click the **Text** option button and type your phrase in the **Signature** text box.

Next Step

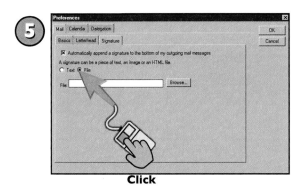

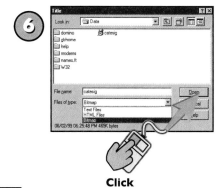

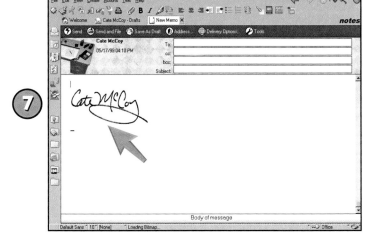

⑤ For an image file or an HTML file, select the **File** option button, then click the **Browse...** button to locate and select the file.

⑥ Find and select the file you want to use as your signature, and click the **Open** button. Then click **OK** to save your Notes signature.

⑦ The signature appears at the bottom of each email message you send.

✓ **Browsing for a File**
Be sure to change the file type to whatever is appropriate using the drop-down list so that you can locate your file.

✓ **File Locations**
By default, Notes browses for files by starting in the Notes directory. Use the **Look in** drop-down list to change this if necessary.

You can create a form letter to quickly reuse a memo in the same format and with the same recipient list. In Notes, this is called *stationery*. Stationery is different from letterhead. Letterhead is the graphic at the top of the emails you write; stationery is a form letter with an addressee list that you can reuse.

Task 17: Creating a Form Letter Using Stationery

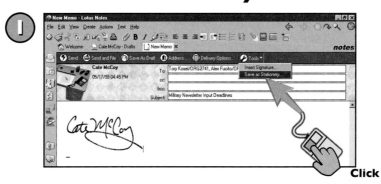

Click

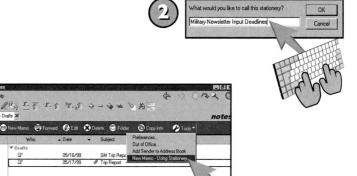

Click

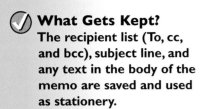

✓ **What Gets Kept?**
The recipient list (To, cc, and bcc), subject line, and any text in the body of the memo are saved and used as stationery.

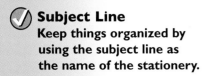

✓ **Subject Line**
Keep things organized by using the subject line as the name of the stationery.

 After you give a new memo a recipient list and a subject, click the **Tools** button and choose the **Save as Stationery** option.

 Type a meaningful name for the stationery (perhaps the same text you typed in the Subject line), and click the **OK** button.

 To use the stationery, from the Inbox click the **Tools** button and choose the **New Memo—Using Stationery** option.

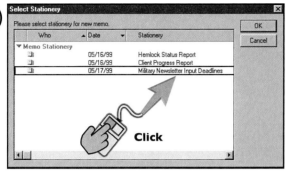

Click

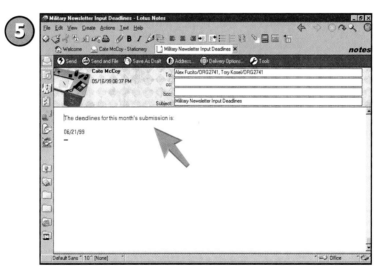

(4) Click the stationery that you want to use, and click the **OK** button.

(5) The stationery appears on your desktop.

Expanding Your Email Repertoire

Lotus Notes R5 has the basic email processing tasks nailed down, but busy people need more. Advanced mail processing power is built into Notes, and Part 3 looks at making those features work for you. Get ready, you're about to become a power user!

Tasks

Task 1: Creating a Mail Rule to Filter Inbound Messages

Mail rules filter and process incoming email messages automatically—for example, grouping messages with a certain keyword in the subject into a folder. You tell Notes what to do, and it handles the mail as it arrives.

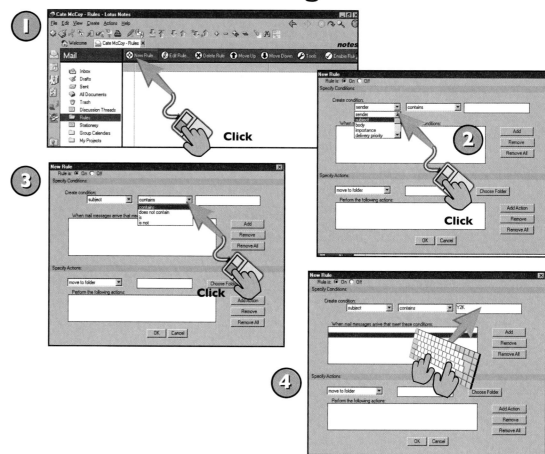

✓ **Additional Conditions**
Rules can have multiple conditions at the same time—for example, moving mail to a folder that comes from your boss and contains a particular keyword in the subject.

✓ **Conditions and Exceptions**
You can specify a rule that will work on a condition except under certain criteria—for example, moving mail to a folder that comes from your boss *except* when it contains a particular keyword.

① In the Rules system folder in the mail database, click the **New Rule** button on the button bar.

② Click the first **Create condition** drop-down arrow, and choose an area of the memo to monitor (for instance, subject).

③ Click the second drop-down arrow, and choose a match criteria action.

④ Type a match criteria in the large text box.

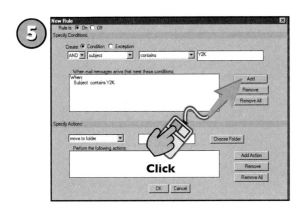

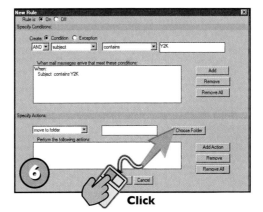

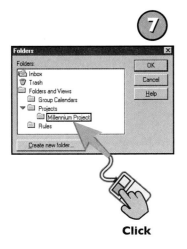

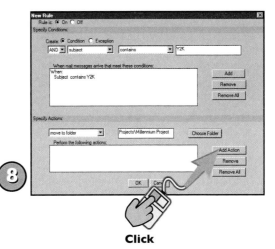

Click

Click

Click

Click

✅ **Changing a Rule**
Use the **Edit Rule** button to change a rule's condition or action after you've created it.

✅ **Removing a Condition**
Click a condition in the **Conditions Edit** box or an action in the **Action Edit** box, and then use the **Remove** or **Remove All** buttons.

✅ **Filtering Out Spam Mail**
You can block unwanted mail from a particular Internet domain by specifying it as a condition and then setting the action to be **Delete the Incoming Message.**

5 Click the **Add** button to add the criteria to the rule.

6 Click the **Choose Folder** button in the Specify Actions area.

7 Select a folder (in this case, **Millennium Project**) from the list, and click the **OK** button.

8 Click the **Add Action** button, and then click **OK** to save the new rule. This rule moves all new email with Y2K in the subject into the Millennium Project folder.

End Task

Task 2: Changing the Execution Order of Mail Rules

If you create several mail rules, they will execute in the order listed in the Rules system folder, top to bottom. To change this order, use the **Move Up** and **Move Down** buttons.

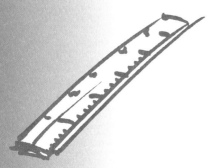

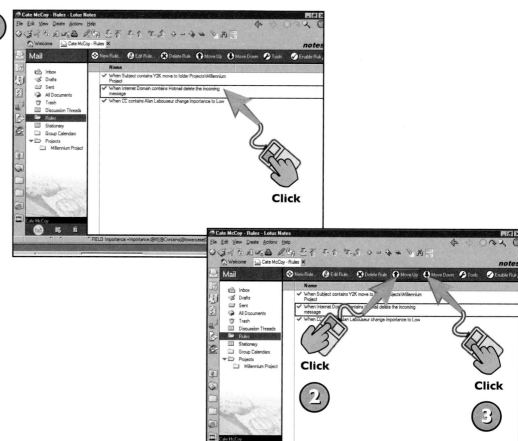

Click

Click

Click

 When Multiple Rules Apply
If multiple rules apply to the same email message, they are applied in order from top to bottom.

 Testing Your Rules
Be sure to test your rules by sending email to yourself that meet the criteria. This is especially important if the rule deletes an email!

In the Rules system folder in the Mail file, click the second rule in the **View** pane.

Click the **Move Up** button on the button bar to move a rule up one position.

Click the **Move Down** button to move a rule down one position.

Task 3: Turning Mail Rules On and Off

Start Here

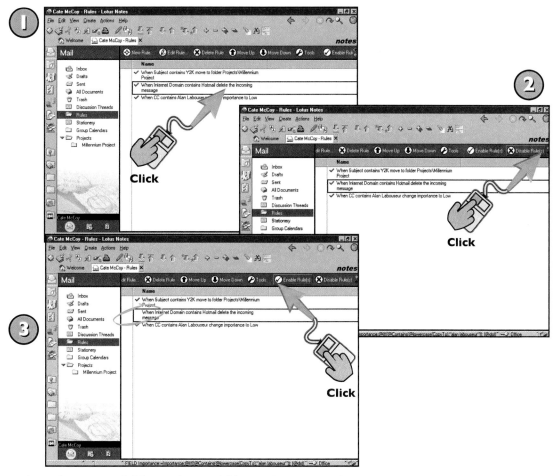

Click

Click

Click

You may want some rules to execute only when you're on vacation, and others only when you're in the office. Control which rules execute by turning them on or off from the button bar.

In the Rules system folder in the Mail file, click a rule in the View pane.

Click the **Disable Rule(s)** button (you may need to click the right-pointing arrow on the far-right side of the button bar to display this button).

The rule is disabled (you can tell because its check mark is removed). Click the **Enable Rule(s)** button to activate a disabled rule.

✓ **Resizing the Panes**
To see all the buttons at one time, drag and drop the border between the Navigator pane and the View pane to the left.

✓ **Editing a Rule**
Rules can also be turned on and off by editing the rule and using the option buttons.

End Task

Task 4: Enabling the Out of Office Agent

Lotus Notes agents are automation modules that perform tasks for you. The Out of Office agent notifies people that you are away after they've sent you emails.

Start Here

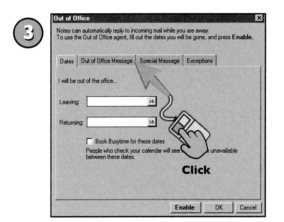

Click

✓ **Special Messages**
You can create one out of office message that is different from the default message. Use the **Special Message** tab to write the message and specify the group of people who will receive the message.

(1) In the Rules system folder in the Mail file, click the **Tools** button in the button bar and choose the **Out of Office** option.

(2) Click the calendar icons to specify the dates when you'll be leaving and returning to the office.

(3) Click the **Out of Office Message** tab, and change the default message if you like.

Next Step

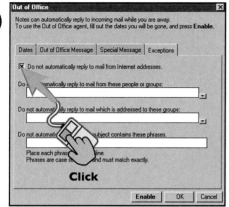

Click

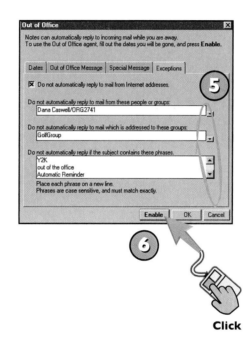

Click

 Endless Loops!
Include the phrase *out of the office* in the area for typing phrases. This will prevent your agent from responding to other peoples' out of office agents!

 Click the **Exceptions** tab, and select the **Do not automatically reply to mail from Internet addresses** check box.

 Use the drop-down arrows to control how the agent behaves for certain groups of people, and the keywords area to limit automatic replies based on message subjects.

Click the **Enable** button to turn on the Out of Office agent.

 Disabling Out of Office
After the agent is enabled, the Enable button changes to Disable. Click it to discontinue the out of office notices, answering yes to all questions along the way.

End Task

Task 5: Delegating Your Email

Start Here

Take off for Tahiti and let someone else manage your mail! Use the Tools preferences to create a delegation profile, and Notes enables another Notes user to read and send mail on your behalf.

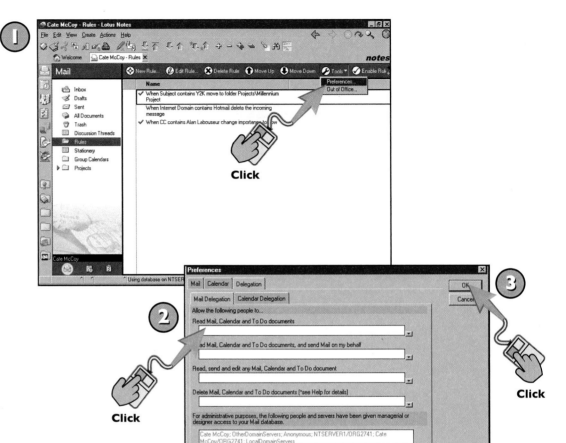

Click

Click

Click

✓ **Delegation Profiles Do Not Expire**
Delegation profiles are not tied to start and stop dates. If you delegate your mail while you're on vacation, remember to change the delegation settings when you return.

In the mail file, click the **Tools** button on the button bar, and select the **Preferences** option.

Click the **Delegation** tab and, in the Mail Delegation tab, use the drop-down arrows to select people who can read and send mail on your behalf.

Click **OK** to save the mail delegation profile.

Task 6: Checking Your Spelling

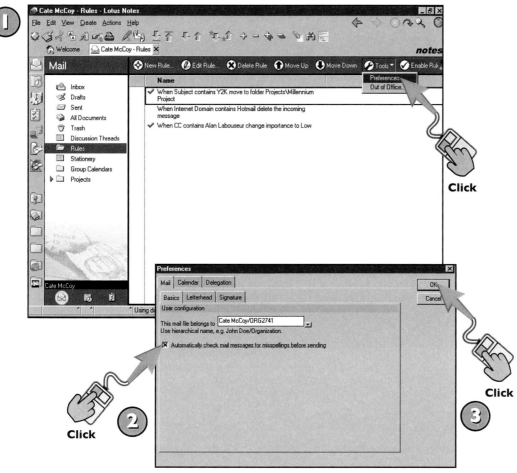

Spell checkers make us all look smarter, and Notes has one built in. You can set preferences so that each time you click the **Send** button to send an email, the spell checker runs automatically.

Click

Click

Click

① Click the **Tools** button on the button bar, and select the **Preferences** option.

② In the Basics area on the Mail tab, click the **Automatically check mail messages for misspellings before sending** check box.

③ Click the **OK** button to save your preferences.

✓ **SmartIcon**
The Edit Check Spelling SmartIcon looks like a book with **ABC** on the cover. Use this button to check the spelling if you don't turn on the automatic checker.

✓ **Delivery Options**
The delivery options in a new memo also let you set an auto spell check option for individual messages.

✓ **Notes Dictionary**
You can add words to the Notes spell check dictionary during the spell check process.

Task 7: Creating a Memo with a Word Processor

Do you prefer Microsoft Word or Lotus Word Pro to the Lotus Notes editor? No problem. You can specify an alternate word processor, and then use it from within Notes through a menu selection. Your preferred word processor is opened within Notes, letting you use it just as you usually do.

✓ **Onscreen Notification of New Mail**
In the User Preferences dialog box on the Mail and News area, click the **Visible notification** check box to enable visible notification of new mail.

✓ **Speed Bumps**
If the alternate word processor is not available on the machine, it can't be used. Special features like replying to a message, attaching a file, and adding a mood stamp are not available outside of the Lotus Notes editor.

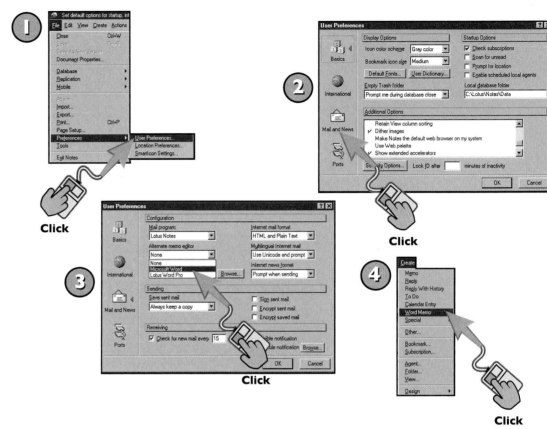

Click

Click

Click

Click

1. Choose **File**, **Preferences**, **User Preferences**.

2. Click the **Mail and News** icon.

3. In the Alternate memo editor drop-down list, select a word processor program, and click **OK** to save your preferences.

4. Choose **Create**, **Word Memo** (if you selected a different word processor in step 3, that program's name appears instead).

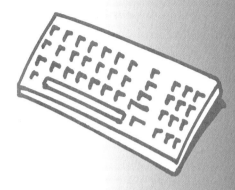

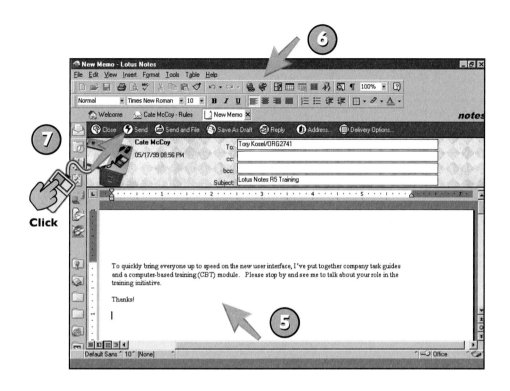

Click

(5) A new memo is opened, featuring a Notes addressing area and button bar as well as a word processing area.

(6) The word processor's (in this case, Microsoft Word) menus and toolbar appear above the Notes addressing area, allowing you full access to its features.

(7) Click the **Send** button on the button bar to mail the memo as you would a normal Notes email.

✅ Receiving Word-Processed Memos
If the person you've sent the word-processed memo to doesn't have that word processor on their machine, Notes displays the text of the message as a normal Notes memo.

✅ Where's the Attachment?
When you receive an email that has been created in Notes using WordPro or Microsoft Word, the Inbox subject line includes the paper clip attachment icon. When you open the email, Notes opens the "attachment" automatically, which is the body of the memo.

Your mail file is the center of activity for much of your work. Organizations often limit the size of mail databases on their servers due to space constraints. If you have available space on your own PC, you can make a local archive copy of your mail file for longer-term storage.

Task 8: Archiving Mail Messages

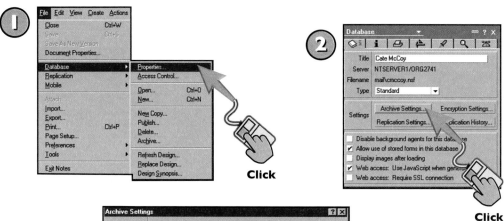

Click

Click

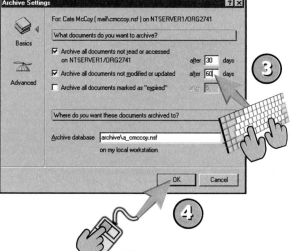

Click

Archive Database Name

By default, the archive database is the same as your mail database but with a prefix of a for archive. You can change this in the archive settings.

Archive Database Location

The archive database is created in a subdirectory folder named `archive` on your local workstation. You can change this default in the archive settings.

From within the **Inbox**, choose **File**, **Database**, **Properties...**.

Click the **Archive Settings...** button.

Set the number of days for archiving purposes to a number that works for you (for instance, archiving unread documents after 30 days and unmodified documents after 60 days).

Click the **OK** button to save your archive settings.

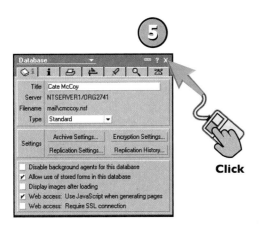

Click

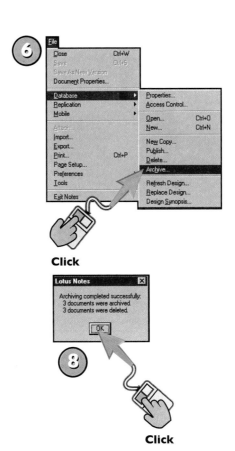

Click

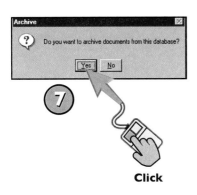

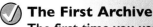

Click

Click

Click

⑤ Click the **Close (X)** button in the **Database** dialog box.

⑥ From within the Inbox, choose **File**, **Database**, **Archive...** to archive mail using your archive settings.

⑦ Click **Yes** to start the archive process to the database specified in your archive settings.

⑧ Be patient while Notes archives your mail, and click **OK** when the archive completion message appears.

✓ **The First Archive**
The first time you use the archive feature, Lotus Notes has to create the archive database, which takes several minutes. You should see the process go faster the second time!

End Task

Lotus Notes does not have to be running to check your email. The Notes Minder feature checks it for you! You activate Notes Minder from the Start menu, which puts an icon in the Windows system tray on the taskbar.

✓ **The Notes Minder Icon**
When new mail arrives, the Notes Minder envelope icon in the system tray changes color. Depending on properties that you set, Notes Minder might also beep at you (you'll set Notes Minder properties in the next task). If the Notes Minder icon is a red envelope, Notes Minder is telling you that you have unread messages in your Inbox. If the Notes Minder icon is a white envelope, Notes Minder is telling you that there are no unread messages in your Inbox. If the Notes Minder icon is a red ×, Notes Minder is having trouble connecting to the server containing your mail database.

Task 9: Starting Notes Minder

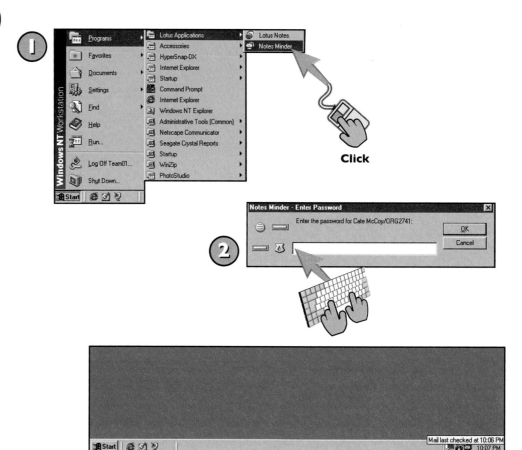

Click

From the Windows desktop, click the **Start** button, select **Programs**, and choose **Lotus Applications**, **Notes Minder**.

Unless Notes is already running, Notes Minder asks you for your Lotus Notes password. Enter it, and click **OK**.

Notes Minder watches for new mail to arrive; float your mouse over the Notes Minder icon in the Windows system tray to see when the mail was last checked.

End Task

Task 10: Setting Notes Minder Properties

Start Here

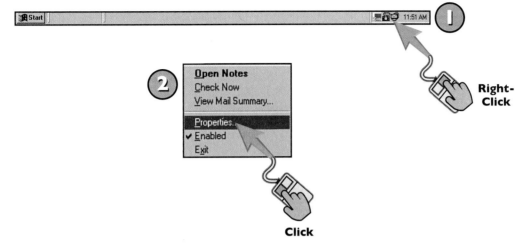

Right-Click

Click

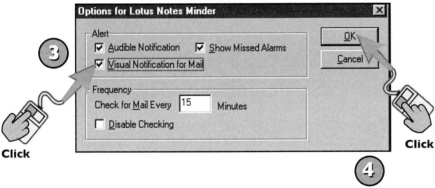

Click

Click

The Notes Minder icon has a context menu to set options like audible alarms and onscreen notification of new mail. You configure these options from the System Tray.

✓ **Frequency**
Checking for mail too often keeps your **PC** and the server processing at a maximum. The default is 15 minutes; anything less may adversely affect server performance.

✓ **Overriding the Frequency**
Use the **Check Now** option in the Notes Minder context menu (right-click the **Notes Minder** icon) to run an immediate check for new mail, overriding the frequency setting.

1. Right-click the **Notes Minder** icon in the System Tray.

2. Choose the **Properties** option.

3. Enable the **Visual Notification for Mail** check box. When new mail arrives, an onscreen message pops up.

4. Click the **OK** button to save your Notes Minder options.

End Task

Task 11: Reading Mail Through Notes Minder

Notes Minder can show you a summary of the unread mail in your Inbox. You select a message from the summary, which launches Notes and displays the message.

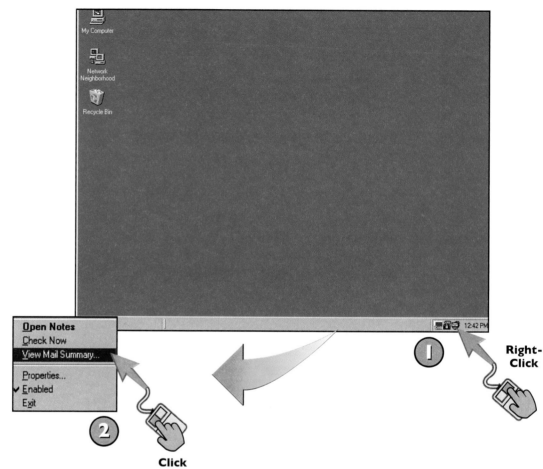

Open Notes
Check Now
View Mail Summary...
Properties...
✔ Enabled
Exit

Right-Click

Click

(✓) **Disabling and Enabling** Right-click the **Notes Minder** System Tray icon and select **Enabled** to switch to disabled mode, which removes the check mark. Click the **Enabled** option again to turn it back on; the check mark appears.

Ⅰ Right-click the **Notes Minder** icon in the System Tray.

② Choose the **View Mail Summary...** option.

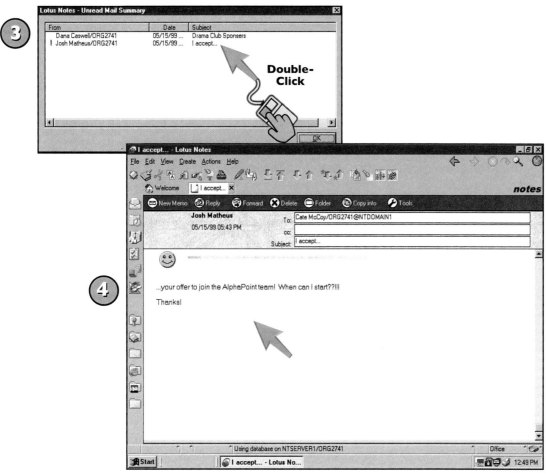

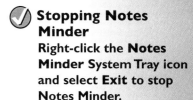

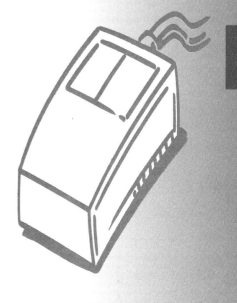

3 Double-click a message in the **Unread Mail Summary** list.

4 Notes Minder launches Lotus Notes (prompting you for your password if Notes is not already running), and opens the mail message you selected.

✅ **Stopping Notes Minder**
Right-click the **Notes Minder** System Tray icon and select **Exit** to stop Notes Minder.

Take Charge of Your Calendar

Busy people demand a powerful electronic calendar to help manage life's activities and time demands. Your personal Lotus Notes calendar is built into the mail database. Features range from basic tasks, such as adding an appointment, to sophisticated concepts, such as group calendaring and scheduling.

In an office environment, sharing your calendar with co-workers streamlines the scheduling process and fosters open communication. This chapter will help you learn techniques and tips to make the calendar a focused, personal activity hub in your day.

Tasks

Task 1: Opening and Closing Your Calendar

The calendar area consists of four views that present different perspectives on calendar information: **Calendar, Meetings, Group Calendars,** and **Trash.** The **Calendar** view is the default, and its information displays in the View pane. You can click **Meetings, Group Calendars,** and **Trash** in the Navigator pane to change the content in the View pane.

✓ **Welcome Page**
The **Basics** Welcome page includes a direct link to the calendar, enabling you to access it by clicking the picture icon or the word **Calendar.**

✓ **Menu Commands**
To close the calendar using the menu, choose **File, Close.** This is the universal way to close windows in Notes.

✓ **The Esc Key**
Pressing the **Esc** key on the keyboard is the same as choosing **File, Close.**

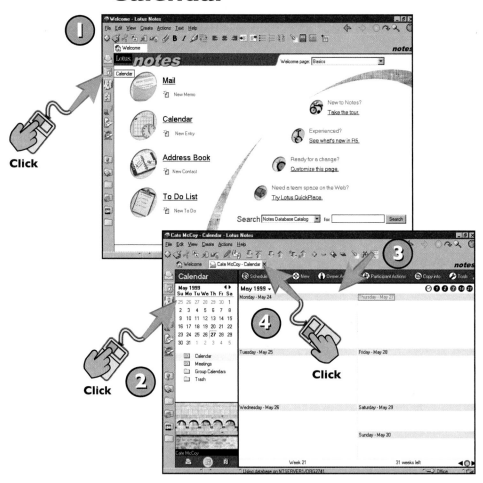

Start Here

Click

Click

Click

1. Click the **Calendar** bookmark on the left border of the Notes screen.

2. The Navigator pane displays a small monthly calendar, which you can click to access different months and days.

3. The View pane shows the details of the calendar for the selected day.

4. Click the **Close (X)** button on the Calendar tab to exit from the calendar.

End Task

Task 2: Setting Start Day Preferences

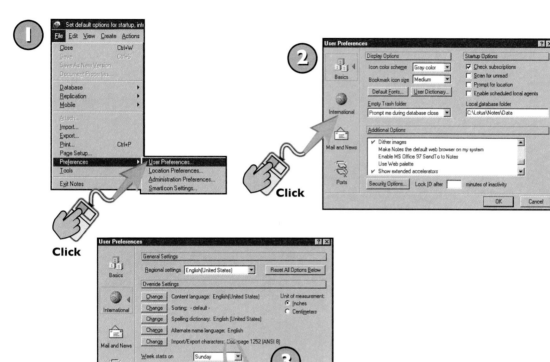

Click

Click

Click   **Click**

Out of the box, **Notes** makes a few assumptions about your calendar preferences. You can customize these preferences to represent your specific needs.

1 From the Notes menu bar, choose **File**, **Preferences**, **User Preferences...**.

2 Click the **International** icon along the left border of the User Preferences dialog box.

3 Use the drop-down arrows to change the day of the week the calendar starts on, displays, and shows in the smaller Navigator pane calendar.

4 Click the **OK** button to save your changes.

 International Flair
The International area of the User Preferences dialog box also enables you to change the English language default for the spelling dictionary and the unit of measure.

Task 3: Configuring Calendar Defaults

You can control several aspects of the calendar and its behavior. The **Tools** button on the button bar in the calendar lets you change key defaults and activate an out-of-office message on days you plan to be away.

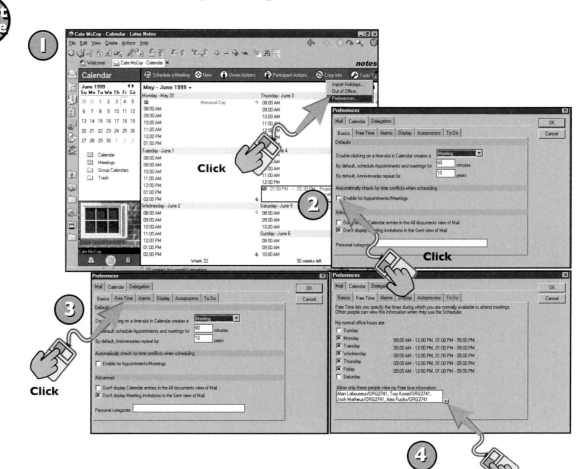

✅ Free Time and Busy Time

To keep track of schedules, Notes uses the phrases *Free Time* and *Busy Time*. Free Time is time when you are normally available for meetings. Busy Time is time that has been scheduled already.

✅ Working 9 to 5

If your work schedule is not Monday through Friday, 9 to 5, change the options using the check boxes and typed time schedules on the **Free Time** tab. The information on this tab is used by Notes and other users to check whether you are available for a meeting.

1 From the button bar in the calendar area, click the **Tools** button and choose the **Preferences...** option.

2 On the Basics tab of the calendar preferences, click the **Enable for Appointments/Meetings** check box to enable conflict checking when scheduling appointments and meetings.

3 Click the **Free Time** tab.

4 Use the drop-down arrow to limit who can see your calendar's free time. By default, every Notes user can see your calendar's free time, but not its entries.

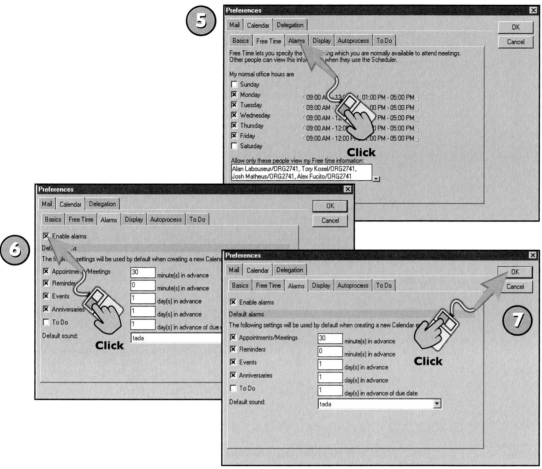

⑤ Click the **Alarms** tab to enable alarms to sound or display for an individual calendar entry.

⑥ Click the **Enable alarms** check box. Activate alarms for each of the different types of calendar entries, setting appropriate time frequencies for each one.

⑦ Click **OK** to save the changes you've made to the calendar preferences.

✓ Autoprocessing Meetings
The **Autoprocess** tab enables you to set a default for how to handle meeting invitations including whether they are deleted from your Inbox after you respond to them or whether they appear in your Inbox at all.

Task 4: Navigating the Calendar

The week-at-a-glance calendar is displayed in the View pane by default. You can change this to show the current day, two days at a time, two weeks at a time, and the full month. The current month is always displayed in the Navigator pane.

✓ **Counting Down**
The last line in the View pane shows calendar countdown information. When the one-day or two-day calendar is onscreen, the number of days since January 1 and the number of days until December 31 are displayed. When the one-week or two-week calendar is shown, the current week number and number of remaining weeks displays. With the month-at-a-glance view, the current month number and number of months remaining displays.

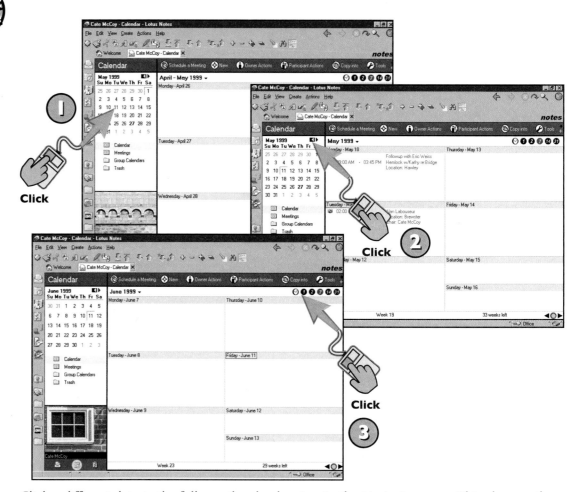

Start Here

Click

Click

Click

① Click a different date in the full-month calendar view in the Navigator pane. This changes the currently highlighted day in the Navigator pane and the View pane.

② Click the left or right arrow in the full-month calendar view in the Navigator pane to move forward or backward one month at a time. This changes what displays in the View pane.

③ Click the **I** button to change the View pane to change to the single day view.

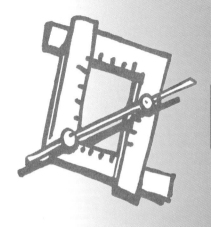

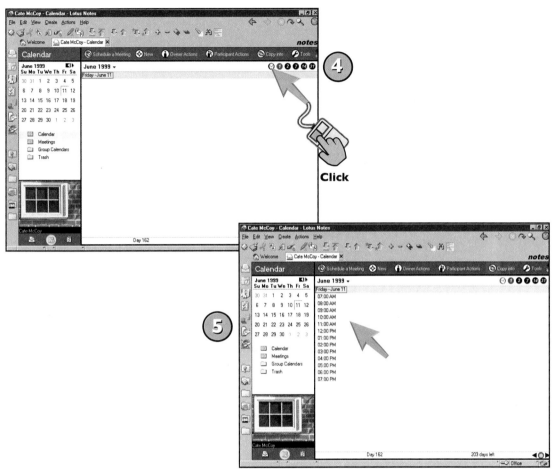

Click

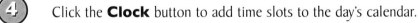

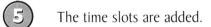

④ Click the **Clock** button to add time slots to the day's calendar.

⑤ The time slots are added.

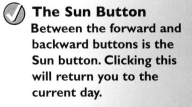

✅ **Forward and Backward**
Use the left and right arrows at the bottom-right corner of the calendar to move through the calendar one day at a time, two days at a time, one week at a time, two weeks at a time, or one month at a time.

✅ **The Sun Button**
Between the forward and backward buttons is the Sun button. Clicking this will return you to the current day.

Task 5: Scheduling a Meeting on Your Calendar

You can add a new meeting to your calendar via any of the calendar views using the buttons on the button bar.

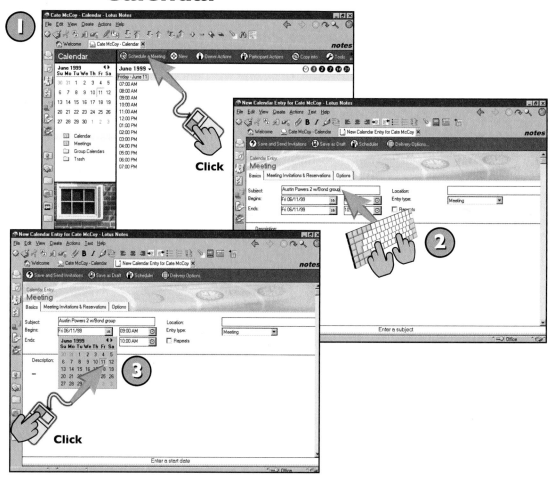

Start Here

Click

Click

①

②

③

 Meeting Description
You can type a long description at the bottom of the calendar entry. This will not show up on the calendar directly, but you can double-click the calendar entry to see its complete details including the description.

 Multi-Day Meetings
Notes sets the start and end dates to the same day. For meetings that span more than one day, use the date-picker for the **Ends** selection to choose a different ending date.

① Click the **Schedule a Meeting** button on the button bar.

② In the **Subject** area, type a short subject that will display in the calendar entry.

③ Click the **Date picker** button next to the Begins field, and then click the meeting's date. (Use the left and right arrows to change months if needed.)

 Next Step

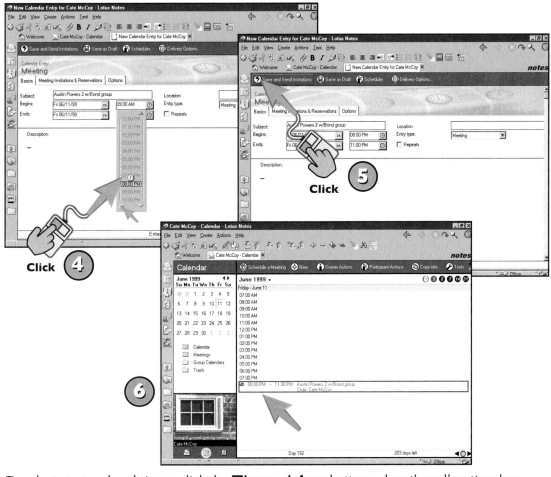

4 To select start and end times, click the **Time picker** buttons, drag the yellow time bar in the drop-down list to the desired time, and click the green check mark to confirm.

5 Click the **Save and Send Invitations** button to add the entry to your calendar.

6 The entry is added.

✅ **Canceling a Meeting**
To cancel a meeting and have Notes automatically notify attendees, use the **Cancel** option in the **Owner Actions** area.

✅ **Deleting a Meeting**
To delete an existing meeting, click its entry and press the **Delete** key and then the **F9** key on the keyboard. This is the same method you used to delete email messages.

✅ **Default End Time**
The default end time is one hour from the chosen start time.

End
Task

Page
71

Task 6: Creating Non-Meeting Calendar Entries

An entry in the calendar can be a meeting, appointment, an all-day event, an anniversary, or a reminder. Meetings are the most popular, so they have their own button. To schedule any of the other types of entries, use the **New** button.

✓ Changing an Entry Type

You can change an entry type when you're looking at the entry details. Use the **Entry type** drop-down arrow to make the change.

✓ Icons for Entries

Each type of entry displays a different icon on the calendar. Meetings have a pair of hands shaking; reminders have a finger with a ribbon tied around it; appointments have a person waving an arm in the air; and all-day events are marked with a lightening bolt at the beginning of the day.

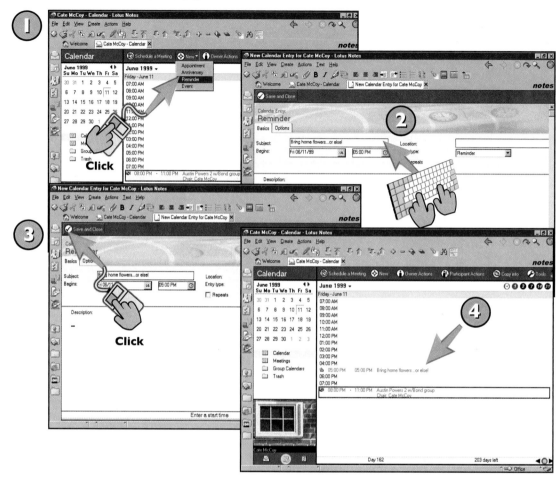

1. Click the **New** button on the button bar and select **Reminder** from the menu.

2. Type a subject, set a date and time, and add a description.

3. Click the **Save and Close** button.

4. The reminder is added to your calendar.

Task 7: Importing Company Holidays

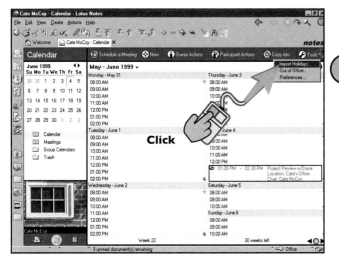

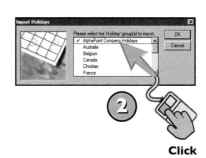

In one step, you can add standard holidays and company-specific holidays to your calendar. There is a central holiday schedule stored on the Domino server so one person can centrally manage holidays for the company.

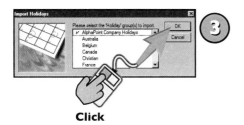

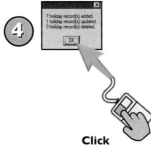

Click

Click

① From within the Calendar area, click the **Tools** button on the button bar and select the **Import Holidays...** option.

② Click a holiday schedule in the list. Several country holiday lists are built into Notes. In this example, AlphaPoint has designated its own holidays.

③ Click **OK** to import the company holidays.

④ You'll see a confirmation message that the holidays were added. Click **OK** to close it.

✅ Holiday Groups
Your company may have its own set of holidays and may even have a different holiday calendar by job function—for instance, administrative staff and sales people. The Domino System Administrator is responsible for setting up the holiday list.

Task 8: Repeating a Calendar Entry

So you're in the doghouse and have made a vow to yourself to bring home flowers every Friday for the next year. To help you remember, use a repeating calendar entry. All calendar entries can be repeated.

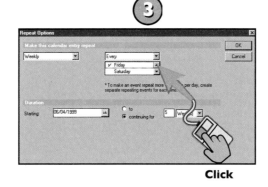

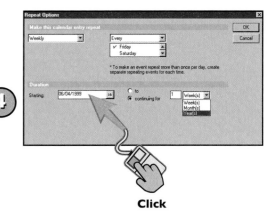

Click

Click

Click

Click

✓ Making Changes to a Repeating Entry

A **Settings** button appears on all calendar entries that are set to repeat. Use this button to change the repeat frequency and duration.

① While creating the reminder entry, click the **Repeats** option. (Refer to Task 6, "Creating Non-Meeting Calendar Entries," to learn about reminder entries.)

② The default settings repeat the calendar entry once a day. Click the drop-down list to change to a different frequency (in this case, **Weekly**).

③ Use the spin box to specify the day of the week on which the reminder should be sent (in this example, **Friday**).

④ In the Duration area, click the **Date** button to choose a starting date.

Next Step

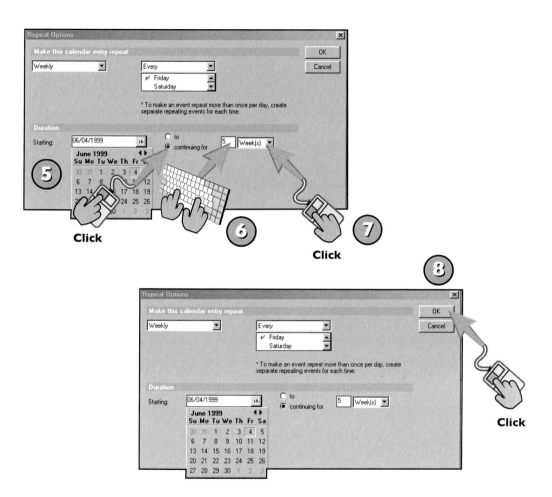

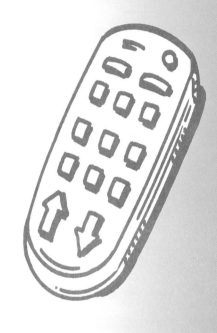

(5) Choose the **to** or **continuing for** radio button to help define the ending date.

(6) Type a number for how many weeks, months, or years the reminder should continue.

(7) Click the drop-down arrow to choose a duration period of either weeks, months, or years.

(8) Click the **OK** button to save your settings.

Task 9: Adding Options and Alarms to an Entry

You can pencil in, categorize, and add an alarm to a calendar entry. The entry gets added to the calendar according to when you pencil it in, but it doesn't prevent other entries from using the same time slot. Marking an entry as **Private** reserves a time slot and prevents other people with access to your calendar from seeing the details of the entry.

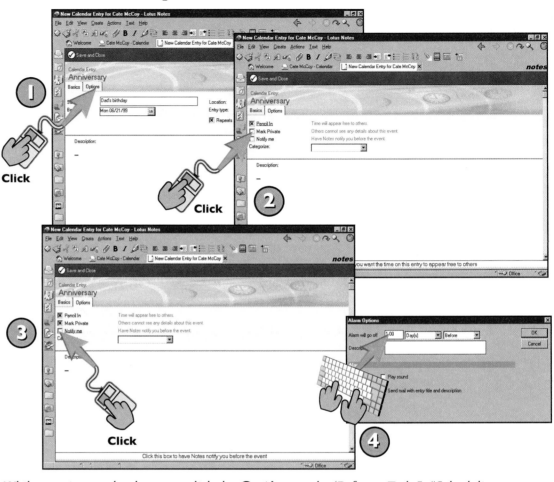

Start Here

Click

Click

Click

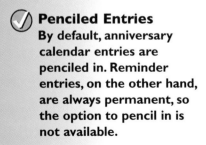

Penciled Entries

By default, anniversary calendar entries are penciled in. Reminder entries, on the other hand, are always permanent, so the option to pencil in is not available.

1. While creating a calendar entry, click the **Options** tab. (Refer to Task 5, "Scheduling a Meeting on Your Calendar," to see how to create a calendar entry.)

2. Click the **Mark Private** check box.

3. Click the **Notify me** option; a dialog box opens, enabling you to set the alarm options.

4. Type the number of minutes, hours, or days prior notification you would like for this event.

Next Step

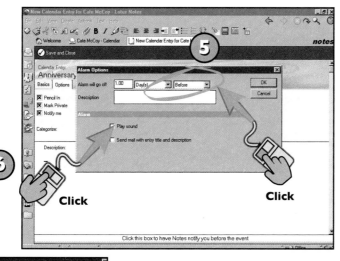

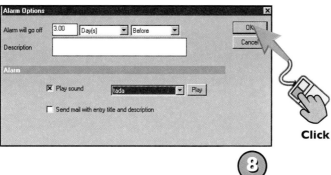

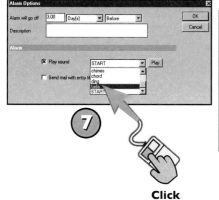

Click

Click

Click

Click

(5) Click the drop-down lists to specify minutes, hours, or days, and whether the alarm should go off before or after the calendar entry date and time.

(6) Click the **Play sound** check box.

(7) Click the drop-down list and select a sound from it.

(8) Click **OK** to save the alarm settings for this calendar entry.

 Play a Sound
When you mark the option to play a sound, the Play button appears and lets you test the sound to make sure you like it.

 End Task

Task 10: Inviting People to Your Meeting

Your personal calendar is stored in your mail file. This integration lets you send and receive meeting notices through the mail.

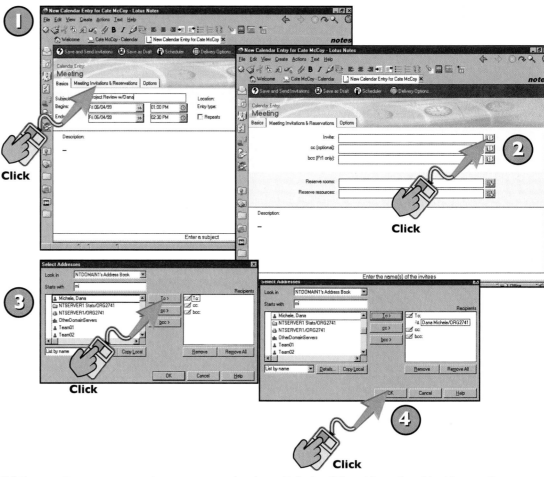

✓ **Color Coding**
The times on a calendar are color-coded. Free time is displayed in white. Busy time is in blue. Time slots with a conflict display in red.

1 While creating a new meeting on your calendar, click the **Meeting Invitations & Reservations** tab. (Refer to Task 5 for help on adding a new meeting to your calendar.)

2 Click the **Picture** icon next to the Invite text box to open the Address Book.

3 You address meeting notices in the same manner as email messages: Select people from the list on the left, and click the **To>** button to add them to your invitation list.

4 Click **OK** to save the list of meeting invitees.

Next Step

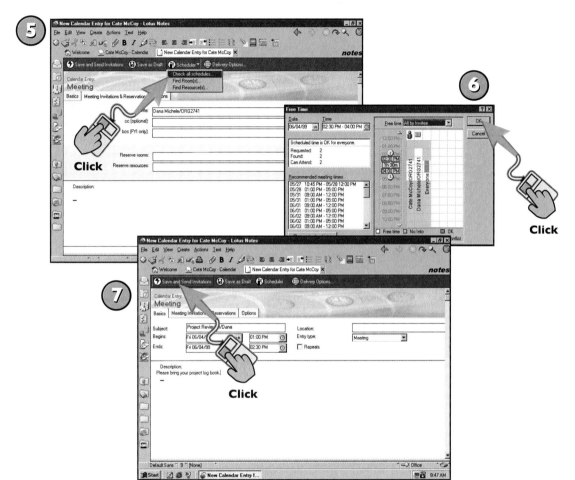

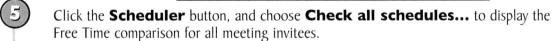

(5) Click the **Scheduler** button, and choose **Check all schedules...** to display the Free Time comparison for all meeting invitees.

(6) If the scheduled time is OK for everyone, click the **OK** button to close the **Free Time** window.

(7) Click the **Save and Send Invitations** button.

✓ Rooms and Resources
Rooms and resources for your organization can be added by someone with the proper authority, usually the Domino System Administrator. After rooms and resources are added to the system, use the icon to schedule the use of a resource for your meeting.

End Task

Task 11: Using the Meeting Scheduler

Notes has a sophisticated scheduler built-in to help you coordinate meetings. Your calendar tracks free time and busy time, and makes this information available to people you've authorized to view your calendar. You can check the schedules for people as you're creating the meeting or after it already exists.

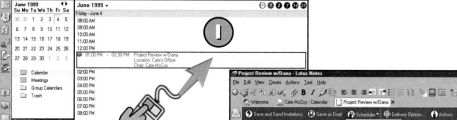

Double-Click

Click

Click & Drag

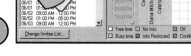

Click

(✓) **Date and Time Pickers**
You can also change the meeting date and time using the date and time picker buttons towards the top-left corner of the **Free Time** window.

(1) Double-click an existing meeting that has invitees to display the meeting details.

(2) Click the **Scheduler** button and select the **Check all schedules...** option.

(3) The Free Time window tells you whether the invitees are free at the requested time. Drag the **start** and **end** time bars to a time slot that is open on everyone's calendar.

(4) Click the up and down arrows on the time slot list to show a different range of times.

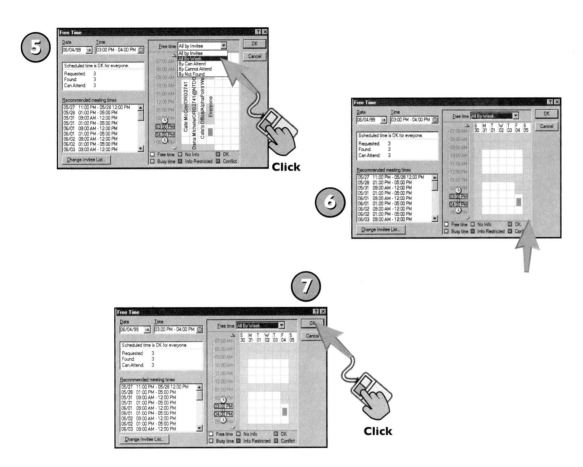

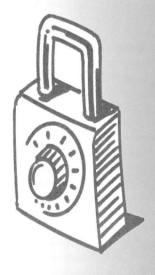

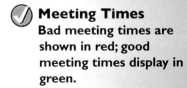

<table>
<tr><td>5</td><td>Open the Free time drop-down list and choose All By Week.</td></tr>
</table>

5   Open the **Free time** drop-down list and choose **All By Week**.

6   The meeting you're currently scheduling appears in green, signaling that there is no conflict with other activities.

7   Click the **OK** button to save your changes.

✓ **Meeting Times**
Bad meeting times are shown in red; good meeting times display in green.

Task 12: Sending Email to Meeting Participants

The powerful combination of email and calendar integration is demonstrated nicely with Owner Actions. The Owner Actions button lets you reschedule or cancel meetings and automatically notifies invitees. You can write an email to meeting participants or send a quick confirmation memo to the invitees. You can also check whether an invitee has accepted your meeting invitation.

Start Here

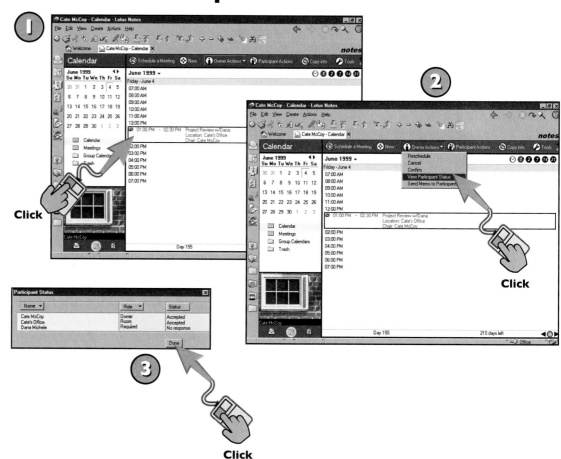

Click

Click

Click

✓ **Sorting the Participant List**
You can sort the **Participant Status** list by name, role, or status by clicking the buttons above the columns.

1 Click a scheduled meeting in your calendar.

2 Click the **Owner Actions** button on the button bar, and select **View Participant Status**.

3 Click the **Done** button to close the Participant list.

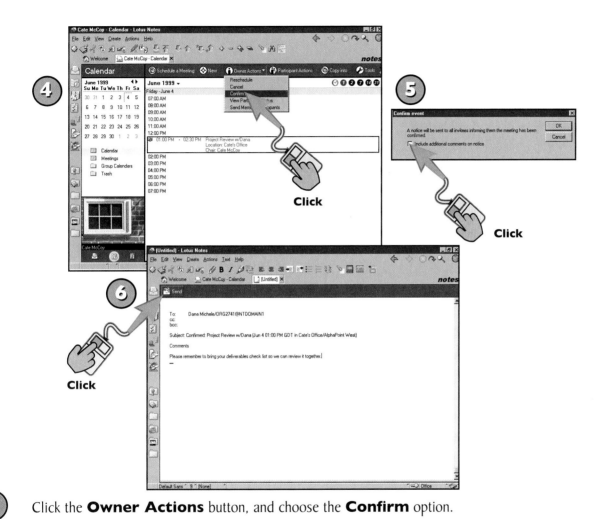

Click

Click

Click

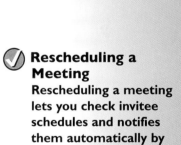

④ Click the **Owner Actions** button, and choose the **Confirm** option.

⑤ Click the **Include additional comments on notice** check box, and click **OK**.

⑥ Type any comments and click the **Send** button to email the confirmation to the invitees.

✅ **Rescheduling a Meeting**
Rescheduling a meeting lets you check invitee schedules and notifies them automatically by email. Room reservations are also rescheduled.

✅ **Additional Comments**
When you confirm a meeting and include additional comments, a typing area lets you write comments back to the meeting initiator.

Task 13: Responding to Meeting Invitations in Your Inbox

Start Here

Just as you can invite people to your meeting, other people can invite you to their meetings. Meeting notices generated by the Notes calendar system are delivered to your Inbox. The subject line will have the word *Invitation* in it together with the meeting subject. You can accept, decline, or delegate the invitation, or propose a new time for it.

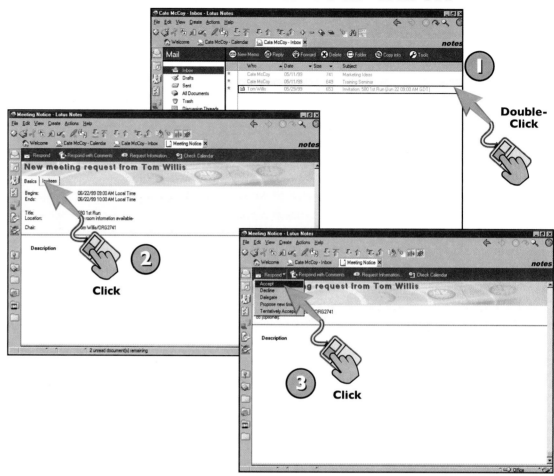

Double-Click

Click

Click

✓ **The Respond Button**
The Respond button only appears on meeting notices in which the sender requires a response. In this case, an Add to Calendar button also appears so that you can proactively decide to attend the meeting.

✓ **Tentatively Accepting**
If you choose **Tentatively Accepting**, an email is sent to the person chairing the meeting with a banner at the top saying that you have tentatively accepted. The meeting is still added to your calendar.

① From the mail file Inbox, double-click an **Invitation** to open it.

② Click the **Invitees** tab to see who else is involved in this meeting.

③ Click the **Respond** button on the button bar, and select **Accept**, **Decline**, **Delegate**, **Propose new time**, or **Tentatively Accept** (I've chosen **Accept**).

Next Step

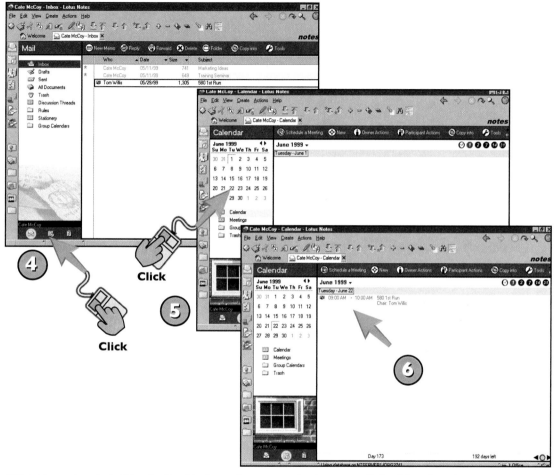

Thumbs Down
When you decline or delegate a meeting, a thumbs down icon is displayed next to the meeting notice in your Inbox. In both cases, the chairperson of the meeting is notified automatically by return email.

Proposing a New Time
Clicking the **Propose new time** option displays a screen that lets you pick an alternate date and time, which is then emailed back to the chairperson of the meeting.

Delegating Meetings
If you select the **Delegate** option under the **Respond** button, you'll see a dialog box with the drop-down list featuring delegate candidates (from the **Address Book**) that you can choose from. Select a name from the list, click **OK** to confirm your choice, and click **OK** again to delegate the meeting.

(4) Click the calendar's **Task Switcher** button at the bottom of the **Navigator** pane to open the calendar.

(5) Click the scheduled day of the meeting invitation. In this example, it was June 22, 1999.

(6) The meeting has been added to your calendar from your Inbox.

Task 14: Working with Group Calendars

Coordinating schedules with other people is hard. To make things a bit easier, Notes lets you create group calendars for people with whom you frequently work. This feature is useful for keeping the schedules of departments, shifts of people, and employees.

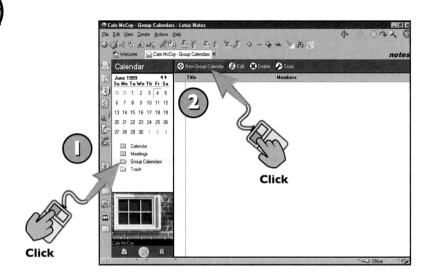

Click

Click

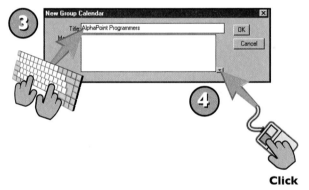

Click

✅ **Conflict Checking**
If a person has not enabled automatic conflict checking for appointments and meetings, his schedule will display in gray as **No Info available.**

✅ **Individual Calendars**
Display any group member's calendar by double-clicking the member's name in the group list.

✅ **Forget the Past**
Group calendars ignore dates in the past and look only at the current day and into the future.

1 In the calendar area of your mail file, click the **Group Calendars** option.

2 Click the **New Group Calendar** button on the button bar.

3 Type a name for the Group calendar.

4 Click the drop-down arrow to add members to the Group calendar.

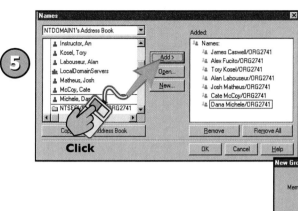

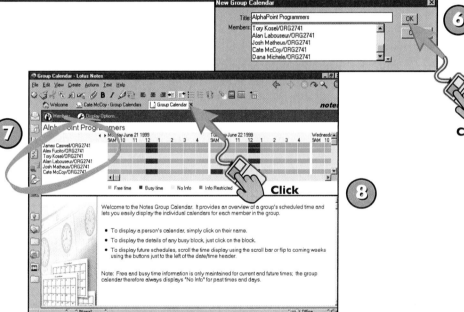

Click

Click

Click

Deleting a Group Calendar
To delete an existing group calendar, select it in the list of group calendars and press the **Delete** key followed by the **F9** key.

Existing Group Calendars
Open an existing group calendar by selecting **Group Calendars** in the Navigator pane, and then clicking the calendar title in the View pane.

(5) Use the **Add>** button to add selected names to the Group calendar one at a time; click the **OK** button when you're finished.

(6) Click the **OK** button to create the Group calendar with the members you've specified.

(7) The Group calendar displays each member's free time and busy time.

(8) Click the **Close (X)** button in the **Group Calendar** window tab to close the Group calendar.

End Task

Prioritize Action Items with the To Do List

Have you ever had a day where you had only one thing that you needed to get done? It never seems to happen that way. The Notes To Do list can help you keep track of all the little things that need to be completed to make a dent in your day. The To Do list is built into the mail file, which means it integrates with your electronic mail and your calendar.

Tasks

Task 1: Creating a New To Do Task

The **New To Do Item** button creates a new task, lets you assign it a priority, and gives it a due date. The subject line should be short enough to put meaningful information on your calendar, while the description area can be as detailed and as long as you like.

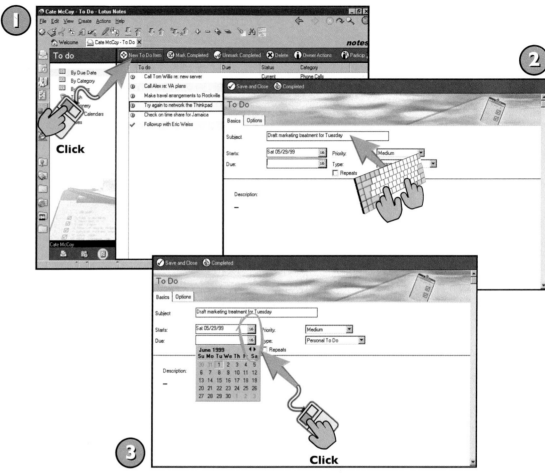

✓ **Personal To Do**
By default, To Do items are meant to remind you of something. These are called *Personal To Do tasks.* The *Group To Do* type is meant to remind a group about a task.

✓ **Creating a Task in the Past**
You can create a task for a date in the past, but you'll see a warning message when you do it just to make sure it's what you really want to do.

① From the To Do list area, click the **New To Do Item** button on the button bar.

② Type a short subject line.

③ Click the date picker buttons to select a start date and a due date.

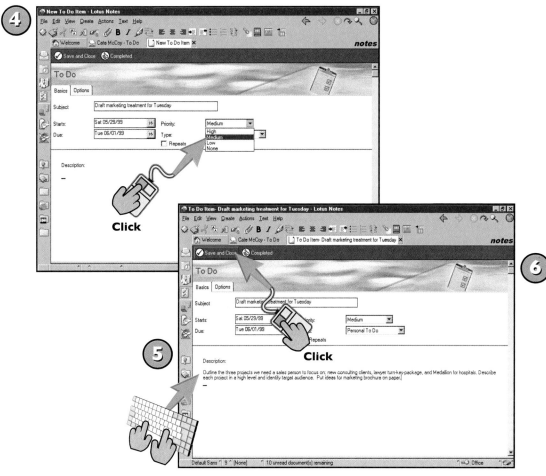

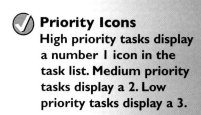

④ Click the **Priority** drop-down arrow and choose a priority for the task from the list.

⑤ Type a description that will jog your memory to the details of what exactly you're supposed to do.

⑥ Click the **Save and Close** button.

✓ Priority Icons
High priority tasks display a number 1 icon in the task list. Medium priority tasks display a 2. Low priority tasks display a 3.

Task 2: Enabling To Do Alarms and Calendar Integration

You can set Notes to sound an alarm or send an email to notify you for individual tasks. First, you must enable To Do alarms in the mail file. If you want To Do tasks to display on your calendar, you need to enable this feature as well.

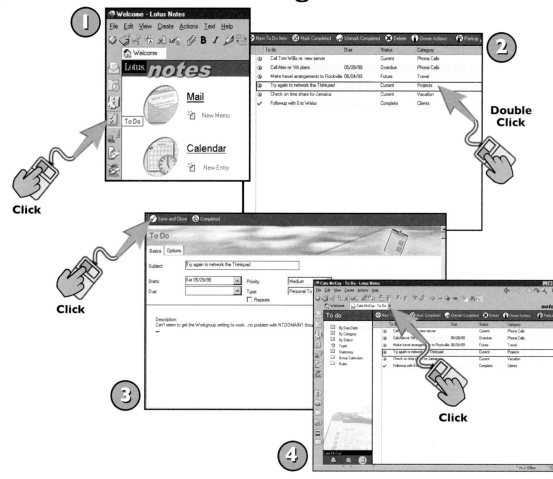

Start Here

Click

Double Click

Click

Click

✓ **Changing Days Notification**
By default, an alarm sounds one day before a task is due. To give yourself more notice, change the option in the Alarms tab by typing in a different number of days.

✓ **Calendar Icons**
If you enable the feature, incomplete tasks display with a check box icon every day until you mark them complete. Past due tasks display with a red exclamation point icon.

1. Click the **Tools** button (you may have to click the right arrow on the button bar to display this button) and choose **Preferences**.

2. Click the **Alarms** tab.

3. Click the **To Do** check box, and then click the **To Do** tab.

4. Click the **Always show current To do's on today's calendar** check box, and click **OK** to save your To Do list preferences.

End Task

Task 3: Opening and Closing the To Do List and Tasks

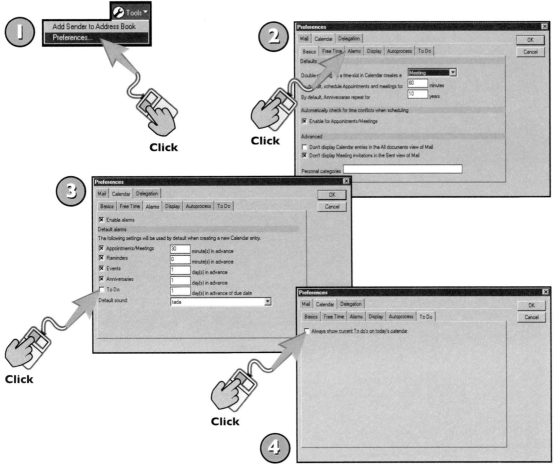

Click

Click

Click

Click

You can access the To Do list from anywhere in Notes. Clicking the **To Do** bookmark jumps you directly into the To Do area. It's also available as a direct link off the **Basics Welcome** page.

✓ **Three To Do Views**
The Navigator pane has three To Do views to choose from: **By Due Date**, **By Category**, and **By Status**. The contents of the By Due Date view are displayed in the View pane by default, and you click the others to switch to a different view.

✓ **Closing Without Saving**
To close a task without saving any changes, use the **Esc** key on the keyboard or choose **File, Close**. If you've made changes, you'll be prompted to make sure you want to exit without saving them.

① Click the **To Do** bookmark to open the To Do list.

② Double-click a task in the list to open it.

③ Click the **Save and Close** button to close a task.

④ Click the **Close (X)** button on the To Do window tab to close the To Do list.

Task 4: Categorizing and Setting Options for a Task

Options for a task include categorizing it, making it private, and setting an alarm. You can categorize a task with one of six categories to act as a quick task organizer. If you've allowed others to see your calendar and it's displaying To Do tasks, you may want to mark the tasks private. Setting an alarm can kick off an audible sound and an email.

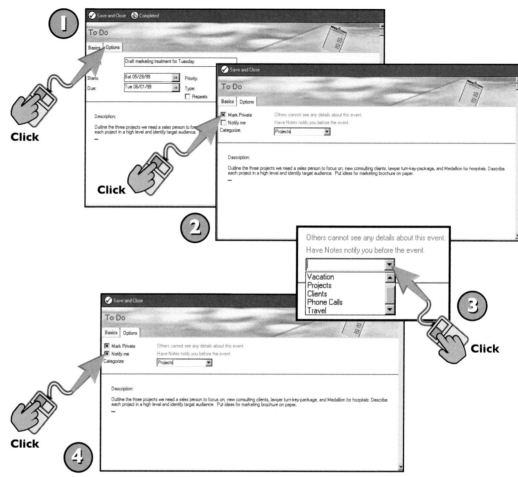

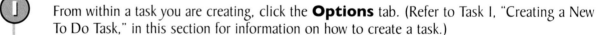

From within a task you are creating, click the **Options** tab. (Refer to Task 1, "Creating a New To Do Task," in this section for information on how to create a task.)

Click the **Mark Private** check box.

Click the **Categorize** drop-down arrow to choose from the six available categories: Holiday, Vacation, Projects, Clients, Phone Calls, and Travel.

Click the **Notify me** check box to enable an alarm for this task.

Next Step

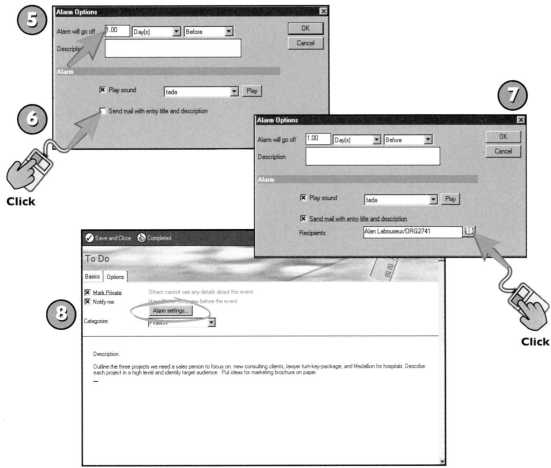

Click

Click

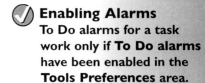

(5) Set the number of minutes, hours, or days the alarm should sound before or after the task is due.

(6) Click the **Send mail with entry title and description** check box.

(7) Click the **Address Book** icon to choose recipients from a list (you can address the reminder to yourself and anyone else), and click **OK** to save the alarm settings.

(8) An **Alarm settings** button is added to your task so that you can change the settings at any time.

✓ **Enabling Alarms**
To Do alarms for a task work only if **To Do alarms** have been enabled in the **Tools Preferences** area.

✓ **Alarm Sounds**
If you previously set an alarm for the calendar or the To Do list, that setting is used as the default.

End Task

Task 5: Repeating a To Do Task

Some tasks in life occur over and over again, like having to pay the electric bill each month. To handle these types of activities, create a repeating task on your To Do list.

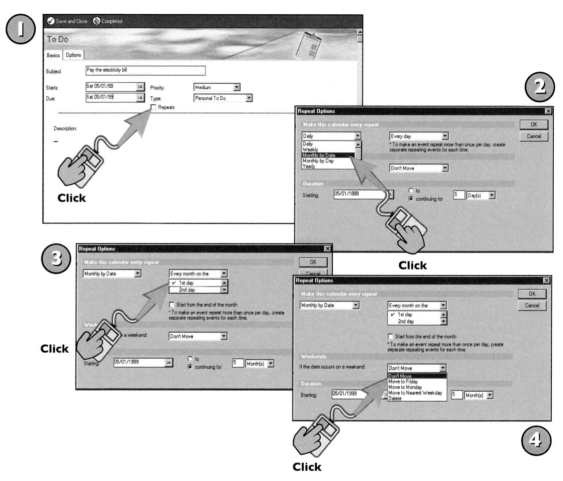

Click

Click

Click

Click

✓ **Last Day of the Month**
To create a repeating entry for the last day of each month, use the **Monthly by Date** and **1st day** options. Then, click the check box option to start from the end of the month.

✓ **Monthly Repeats**
You can set options to repeat the task every other month, every third month, and so on.

✓ **Specific Dates**
The Custom option Repeats frequency lets you enter a specific set of dates to remind you of a task.

① While creating a To Do task, click the **Repeats** check box in the Basics tab. (Refer to Task 3 for more information on creating a task.)

② Click the **Daily** drop-down list to change the repeat frequency. In the case of an electric bill reminder, **Monthly by Date** is a good choice.

③ Select a day of the month from the second drop-down list.

④ In the Weekends area, click the drop-down list to choose an option to control the day to repeat the entry on in case the original date is a weekend.

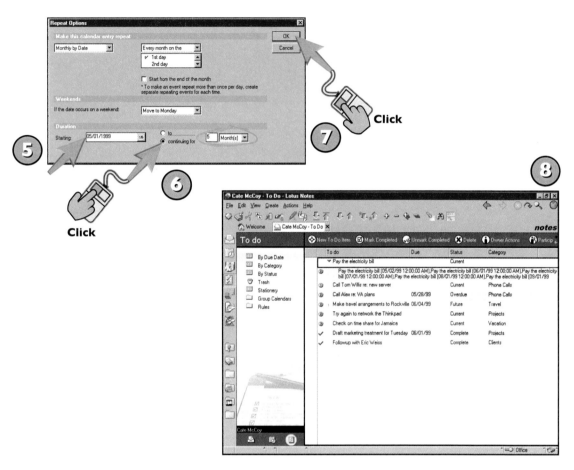

Click

Click

(5) Notes automatically calculates the start date for the repeating entry.

(6) Click the option buttons and use the drop-down list to control when the repeating entry should end.

(7) Click the **OK** button to save your repeating entry.

(8) The repeating entry displays in the View pane with the subject line in a collapsible category. Upcoming dates for the task are displayed as well.

End Task

Task 6: Marking a Task Completed

After a task is completed, you change its status from the To Do list view or from within an individual task. Completed tasks appear with a green check mark on the view with a status of Complete.

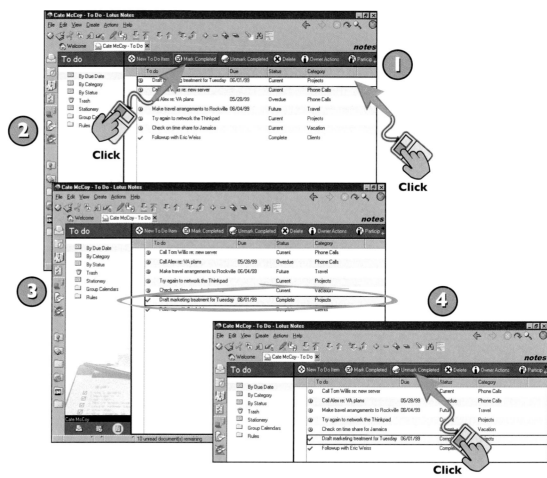

Start Here

Click

Click

Click

✓ **Status Changes**
When you create a task without a due date, it's given a status of Current. Tasks created with due dates in the future are given a status of Future. The status of a task that is uncompleted past its due date is marked as Overdue.

✓ **Deleting Tasks**
All tasks remain on the list until you use the **Delete** button and **F9** key to discard the tasks.

① Click a task in the To Do list area to select it. A black rectangle around the row marks the task as selected.

② Click the **Mark Completed** button on the button bar.

③ The completed task is tagged with a green check mark, and its status is changed to Complete.

④ To change the status of a completed task back to Current, click the **Unmark Completed** button on the button bar.

End Task

Task 7: Assigning a Group To Do Task

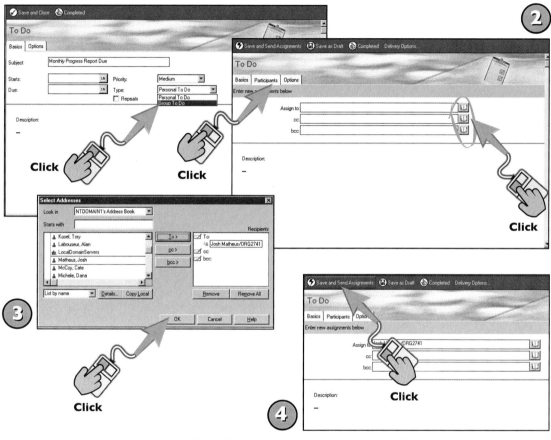

Tasks that you need other people to complete can be tracked by **Notes** through your own **To Do** list. This type of **To Do** task is called a *Group To Do*. Tasks you assign to other people are automatically emailed to them.

✓ Save As Draft
The **Save As Draft** button saves the **To Do** item but does not send it to the participants.

✓ Courtesy Copy
Use the **cc** field to send a copy of the **To Do** task to other people.

✓ Blind Courtesy Copy
The recipient list of the **bcc** field is hidden from recipients on the **To** and **cc** lists.

① While creating a To Do task, click the **Type** drop-down arrow and choose the **Group To Do** option.

② Click the **Participants** tab. In the **Assign to**, **cc**, and **bcc** areas, click the **Address Book** icon to display a list from which you can choose participants.

③ Select names from the list on the left and click the **To** button to add them to your list of participants. When you finish adding participants, click **OK**.

④ Click the **Save and Send Assignments** button.

End Task

Task 8: Setting Delivery Options on Group Tasks

Delivery options can generate additional information for you about the document (like a to do, email, or meeting) that you're sending through email. You can be notified of successful or unsuccessful delivery as well as set a priority. You can attach a return receipt, turn off the ability for participants to reply from within the email, prevent delegation of tasks, as well as counter-proposals on meetings. Security options let you digitally protect the mail with a computerized key.

✓ **Delivery Report**
Notes can notify of a delivery failure if you use the option **Only on failure. Confirm delivery** and **Trace entire path** will send you an email on successful and unsuccessful deliveries with the trace sending a message from every way point server the message travels through on its way to a destination.

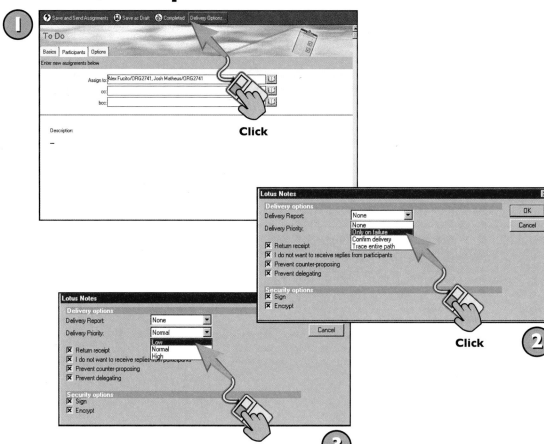

Create a Group To Do task (refer to the last task), but before you save and send it, click the **Delivery Options** button on the button bar.

Click the **Delivery Report** drop-down arrow and select an action to monitor the progress of the To Do mail message.

Click the **Delivery Priority** drop-down arrow, and choose from Low, Normal, or High.

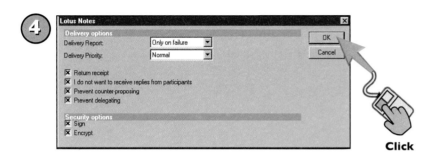

Click

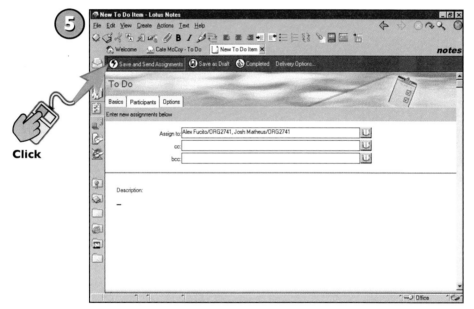

Click

✓ **Which Priority Makes Sense for You?**
High priority tells Notes to send the message immediately. Low priority means the server will wait until off-peak hours to send the message. Normal priority sends the mail according to the server schedule set up for your mail server.

✓ **Security Options**
Notes lets you encrypt or digitally sign email. Encryption prevents people other than recipients from reading the message. Digital signatures guarantee that the mail isn't tampered with during the delivery transmission process. Check out Part 11 for more information on security.

④ Click the **OK** button to save the delivery options.

⑤ Click the **Save and Send Assignments** button to assign the task.

Task 9: Receiving a Task Assigned to You

Tasks assigned to you by someone else appear in your Inbox as an email and in your To Do list. After you've looked over the details of the task as it was sent, you can request additional information from the person who sent the task to you.

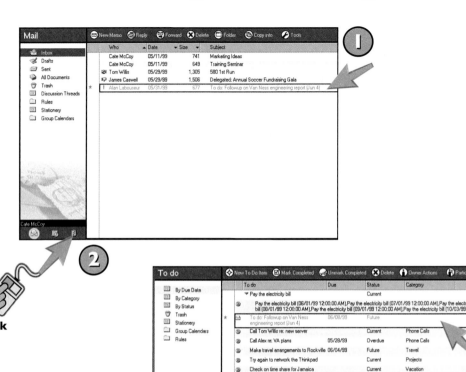

Start Here

Click

Double Click

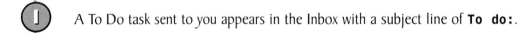

① A To Do task sent to you appears in the Inbox with a subject line of **To do:**.

② Click the **To Do List** button on the task switcher.

③ Double-click the task in the To Do list to open it.

Next Step

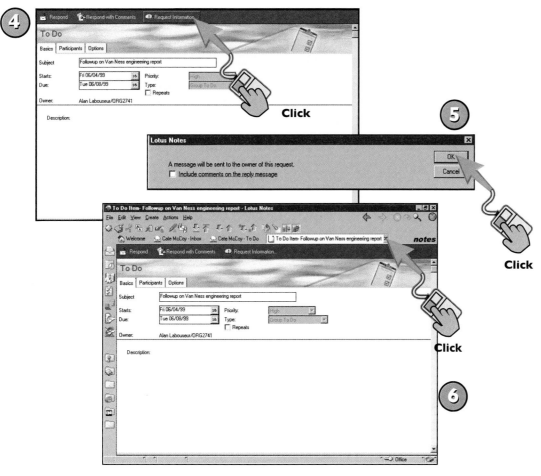

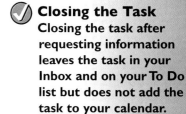

4 Click the **Request Information** button to request details via email (with a banner noting that the request is from you) from the person who assigned the task.

5 Click the **OK** button to send a return message, using the check box to include comments on the reply message if appropriate.

6 Click the **Close (X)** button in the **To Do Item** window tab to exit from the To Do task.

✓ **Closing the Task**
Closing the task after requesting information leaves the task in your Inbox and on your To Do list but does not add the task to your calendar.

Task 10: Adding a Task You've Assigned to the Calendar

Tasks you receive in email that were assigned to you by someone else are not automatically added to your calendar. You have the opportunity to review the task and take an action to accept the responsibility, decline it, or delegate it.

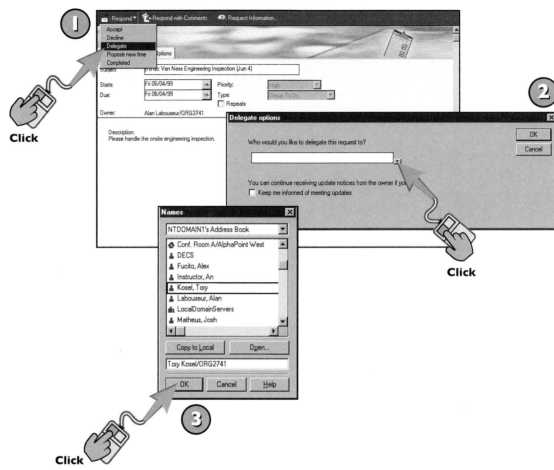

✓ **Delegating To Do Tasks**
If the owner of the task set a delivery option to prevent delegating, the option to delegate a task will not appear on the list of possible responses.

✓ **Respond with Comments**
The **Respond with Comments** option provides the same response options, and lets you send an email back to the person who assigned you the task.

✓ **Accepting**
If you select **Accept**, the task is marked as read and is added to your calendar.

(1) From within a task you've received by email, click the **Respond** button on the button bar and choose **Delegate**.

(2) Click the drop-down arrow to display a list of people to whom you can delegate the task.

(3) Select the delegate name from the list and click **OK**.

Next Step

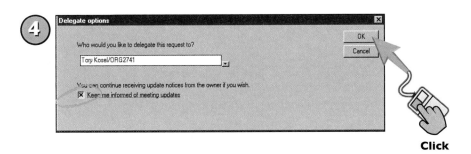

Click

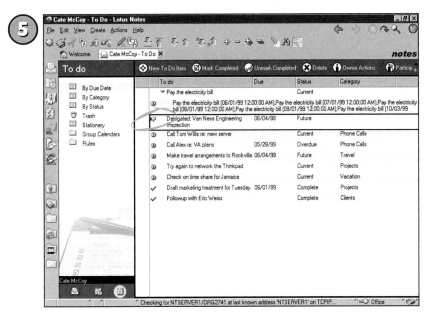

④ Click the **Keep me informed of meeting updates** check box, and click **OK**.

⑤ The thumbs down icon indicates that you have not accepted the assigned task.

Manage Your Personal Address Book

You will use two primary address books frequently in Notes: your personal address book and the server's address book.

Your personal address book tracks the names and contact information for people and organizations that you deal with frequently. The address book is a Notes database stored on your personal computer. You can add any information you like to your personal address book because you own it and are in complete control!

The server's address book tracks information on all the Notes users registered on a particular server. The Domino System Administrator is responsible for maintaining the information in this address book.

Tasks

There may be multiple address books stored on your machine. For instance, in a large company, there could be an entire address book devoted to the sales organization and another just for the manufacturing organization. You need to identify your primary personal address book so that Notes can look there first for information.

Task 1: Determining the Default Address Book

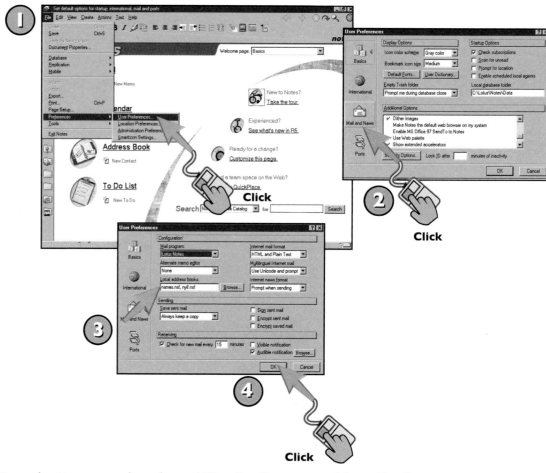

Start Here

Click

Click

Click

Click

✅ **Local Databases**
The term *local* means that the database is stored on your personal computer's hard drive, not on a Domino server.

✅ **names.nsf**
names.nsf is the actual filename for your local Notes address book; *personal address book* is the title of the database.

✅ **What's an NSF?**
In Domino, *NSF* stands for *Notes storage facility*. It is a specific type of computer file that acts as a container for Lotus Notes databases.

1 From the Notes menu bar, choose **File**, **Preferences**, **User Preferences**.

2 Click the **Mail and News** icon.

3 The NSF file listed first in the **Local address books** area is the default, and will be searched first. Other address books listed here are searched in order, left to right.

4 Click **OK** to save your mail and news user preferences.

End Task

Task 2: Opening and Closing the Address Book

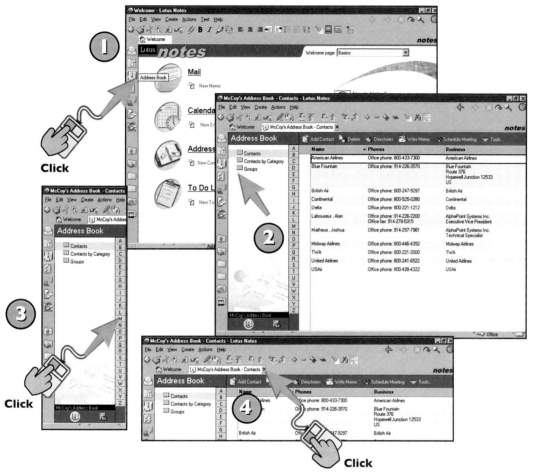

Click

Click

Click

You can access your personal address book from anywhere in **Notes** using the **Address Book** bookmark. There is also a link from the Basics Welcome page to open the address book, and another to add a new contact.

① Click the **Address Book** bookmark.

② The Navigator pane in the Address Book offers three views: Contacts (the default, displayed here), Contacts by Category, and Groups.

③ Click one of the letters between the Navigator pane and the View pane to jump to contacts that start with that letter.

④ Click the **Close (X)** button in the Address Book window tab to leave the Address Book.

✓ **Sorting Contacts**
Click the triangle in the **Name** column heading to sort the contact names in ascending or descending order.

End Task

The heart of your address book is the contact information. This information is entered and saved in several tabs of data. Enter as much or as little information as you like. You can use the **Save and Close** button at any time to save the information.

Task 3: Adding New Contacts to Your Personal Address Book

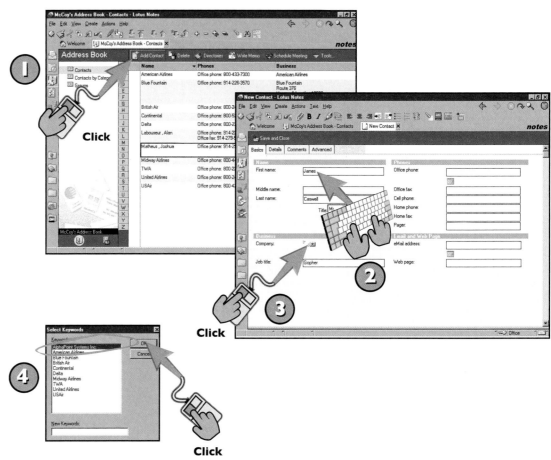

Click

Click

Click

(1) From within the Address Book, click the **Add Contact** button on the button bar.

(2) Type the contact's first and last name into the appropriate areas on the **Basics** tab, filling in as much information as you have available.

(3) Click the **Company** drop-down arrow.

(4) This list represents companies already present in your address book. Select a company from the list or type a new name in the **New Keywords** area, and click the **OK** button.

Next Step

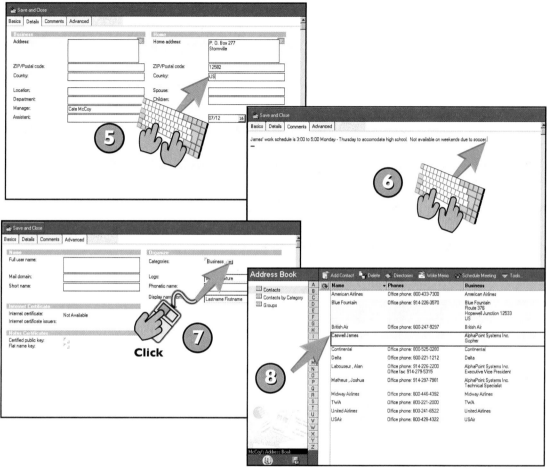

Click

Editing Contact Information
Double-click a contact in the **View** list to open it. It is opened in edit mode, and the **Save and Close** button becomes available.

Deleting Contacts
Select a contact in the **View** list, click the **Delete** button on the button bar, and then press the **F9** key on the keyboard.

Refresh Button
Whenever you see a blue circular arrow in the top-left corner of the View pane, click it to refresh the data being displayed. This re-reads the stored data and updates the onscreen data.

5 Click the **Details** tab, and type business and home address information.

6 Click the **Comments** tab, and type any miscellaneous information you want to record about this contact.

7 Click the **Advanced** tab, choose a category for this contact from the existing list using the drop-down arrow, and then click the **Save and Close** button.

8 The contact is added.

Task 4: Copying Contacts from the Server's Address Book

Typing in contact information is one way of adding to your address book. Another way is to copy it from the server's address book while you're addressing an email.

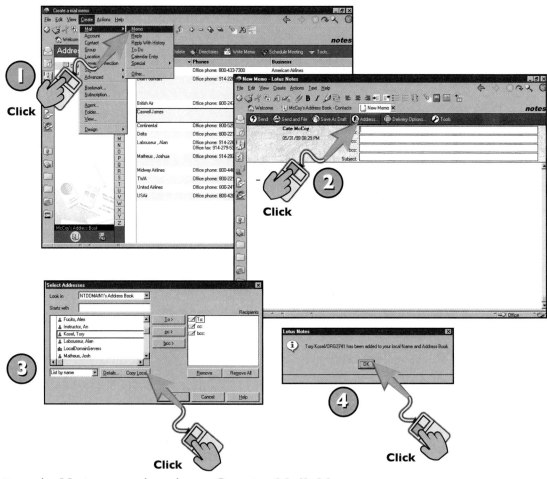

✓ What Gets Copied?
The minimum information in the server's address book includes the first name, last name, and email address.

✓ Maintaining the Address Books
You're in charge of all changes in your personal address book. The system administrator maintains the server's address book. The two don't share information. Changes made in one of the address books won't be updated in the other address book.

① From the **Notes** menu bar, choose **Create**, **Mail**, **Memo**.

② Click the **Address** button.

③ Select a name from the list on the left, and click the **Copy Local** button.

④ Click **OK** to confirm that the entry has been added to your local address book, and continue to write the memo in the usual manner.

Task 5: Categorizing Your Contacts

Start Here

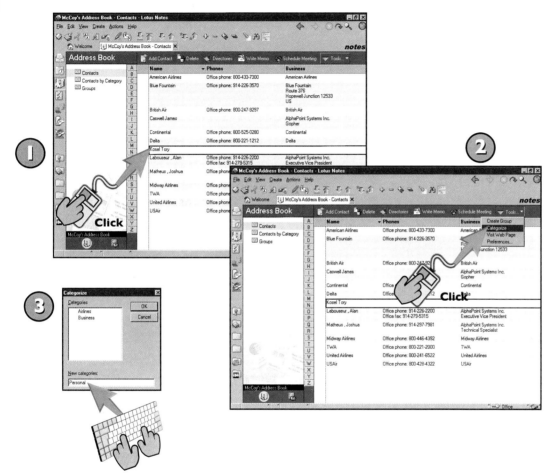

Click

Click

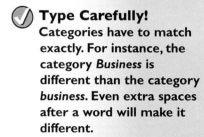

There is no limit on the number of contacts you can add to your address book. To help keep your contacts organized, you can categorize each contact using keywords that you control. The Contacts by Category view in the address book shows you all your contacts sorted into their category; a (Not Categorized) listing means that the contact did not have a category assigned to it.

① Select a contact from the View list.

② Click the **Tools** button on the button bar, and choose the **Categorize** option.

③ Select a category from the list or type a new one, then click **OK**.

Type Carefully!
Categories have to match exactly. For instance, the category *Business* is different than the category *business*. Even extra spaces after a word will make it different.

Task 6: Setting Personal Address Book Preferences

The **Preferences** area of the personal address book lets you personalize the presentation of the address book information to your own tastes. You can set an image to display in each contact, choose a sort order for group names and people names, and specify whether **LDAP** searches can be made into the contents of the Address Book.

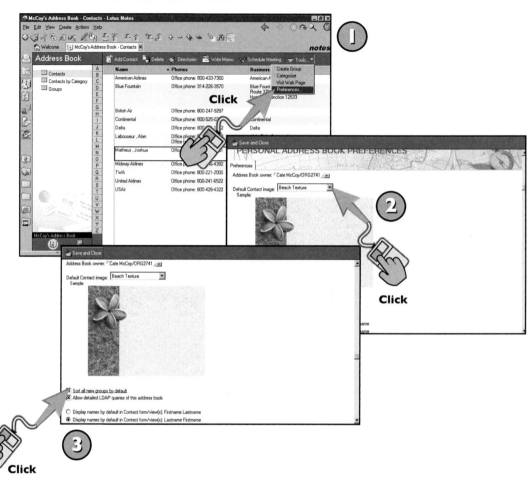

Click

Click

Click

Click

1. From within the Address Book, click the **Tools** button on the button bar and choose the **Preferences** option.

2. By default, the Beach Texture image is displayed with each contact record. You can choose a different image by clicking the drop-down arrow to display additional choices.

3. Click the **Sort all new groups by default** check box, which displays groups in alphabetical order in the Address Book.

Next Step

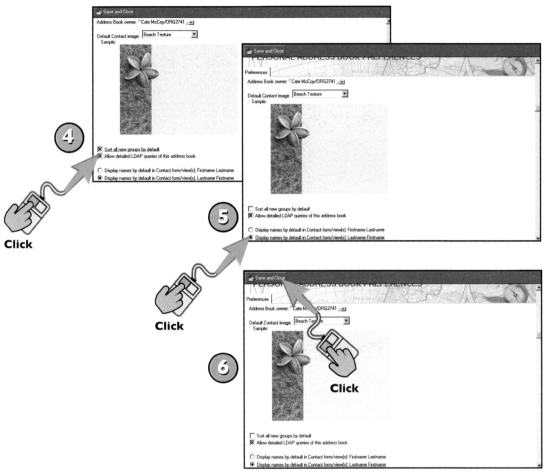

Click

Click

Click

(4) Click the **Allow detailed LDAP queries of this address book** check box if you want your address book to work as a source of information during address lookups.

(5) Click one of the option buttons at the bottom of the window to specify whether entries in the Address Book are displayed by last name or first name.

(6) Click the **Save and Close** button.

 LDAP
LDAP is an acronym for *Lightweight Directory Access Protocol.* **LDAP** is a popular type of Internet directory style used by many software vendors and public Web sites.

Task 7: Working with Directories

Directory is another word for a collection of addresses and contact information. The Notes address books are directories. A directory typically contains a person's name, address, and contact phone information. It may also contain additional information specific to that person. You can look at the directory entries (people) in the server's address book using the **Directories** button in your personal address book.

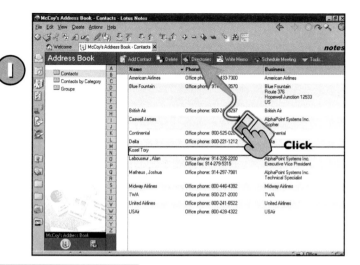

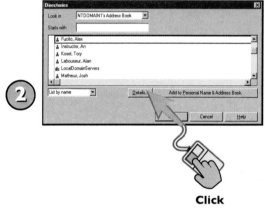

Click

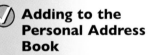

Adding to the Personal Address Book
Any entries you copy to your personal address book will not be updated, because you're the only one who can do that.

 From within the Address Book, click the **Directories** button on the button bar.

 Select a person or a group in the list and click the **Details** button.

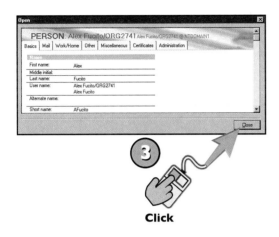

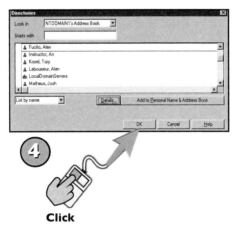

Click

Click

③ The information in the server's address book is presented to you in tabs that you can click to investigate. Click the **Close** button when you're done.

④ Click the **OK** button to close the **Directories** window.

Task 8: Creating and Maintaining a Group

If you collaborate with teams of people, creating groups in your personal address book can help you streamline communications. You can group individual contacts together, give the group a name, and then use the name for memos, To Do tasks, and meetings.

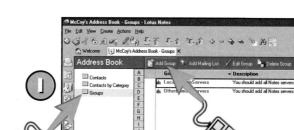

Click

Click

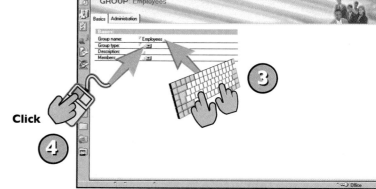

Click

✓ **Group Meeting**
To schedule a meeting with a group, select the group in the **View** list and then click the **Schedule Meeting** button. The Invitee list is automatically filled in for you.

✓ **Sorting the Member List**
While you're creating a new group and after you've added the members, use the **Sort Member List** button to sort the list of names alphabetically.

① Click the **Groups** view in the Navigator pane.

② Click the **Add Group** button.

③ Type a Group name.

④ Click the **Group type** drop-down button.

Next Step

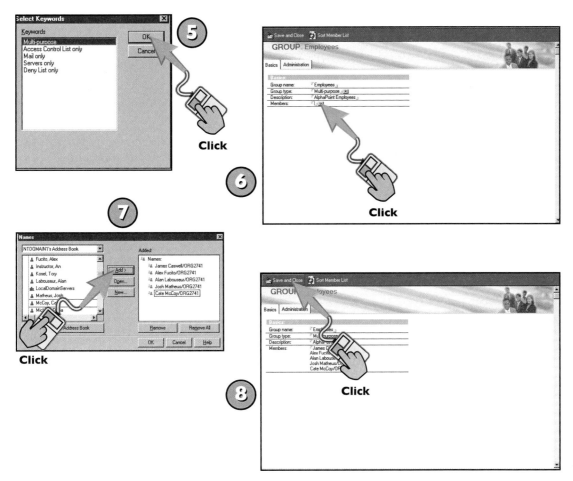

Click

Click

Click

Click

⑤ Choose a group type of **Multi-purpose** or **Mail only** and click **OK**.

⑥ Click the **Members** drop-down arrow.

⑦ Select names from any of the available address books, click **Add**, and then click **OK** when you're finished adding names.

⑧ Click **Save and Close**; the new group is saved.

Task 9: Setting Up a Mailing List

A mailing list in Notes is a set of members collected together and given a group name. Unlike other types of groups in Notes, mailing lists can only be used with email.

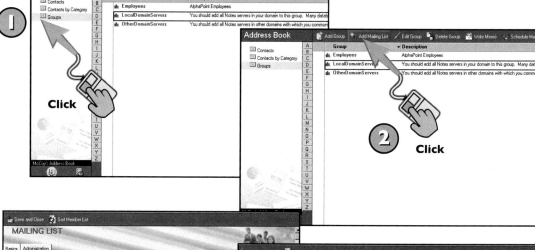

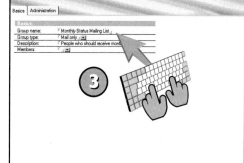

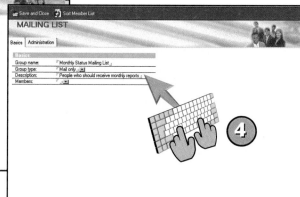

✅ **Mailing List Names**
To easily identify groups that are mailing only, use the word Mail somewhere in the group name.

✅ **Group Memo**
To write a memo to group, select the group in the **View** list and then click the **Write Memo** button. The memo is automatically addressed for you.

① Click the **Groups** view in the Navigator pane.

② Click the **Add Mailing List** button.

③ Type a Group name for the mailing list.

④ Optionally, type a Description for the group.

Next Step

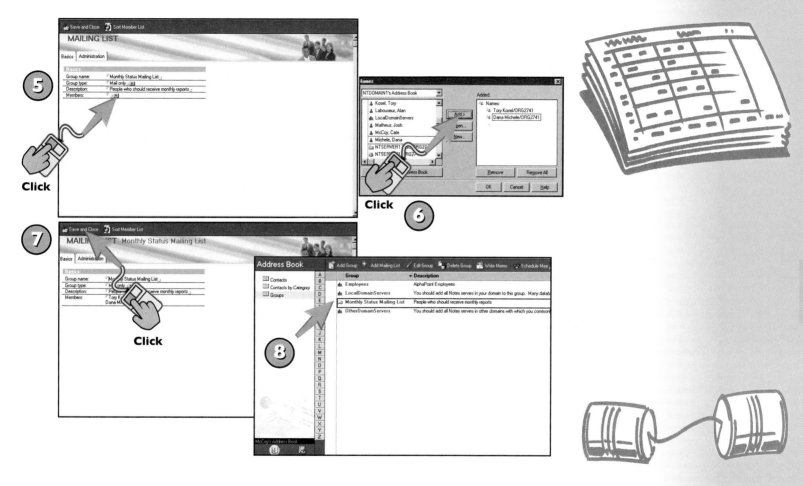

Click

Click

Click

---

5 Click the **Members** drop-down arrow.

6 Select names from any of the available address books, click **Add**, and then click **OK** when you're done adding names.

7 Click **Save and Close** to save the new mailing list.

8 The mailing list displays in the Group View pane with an envelope icon.

After a mailing group list has been created, you can use it to address mail from anywhere in Notes. In this example, we'll create an email directly from the Welcome page.

Task 10: Writing a Memo Using a Mailing List

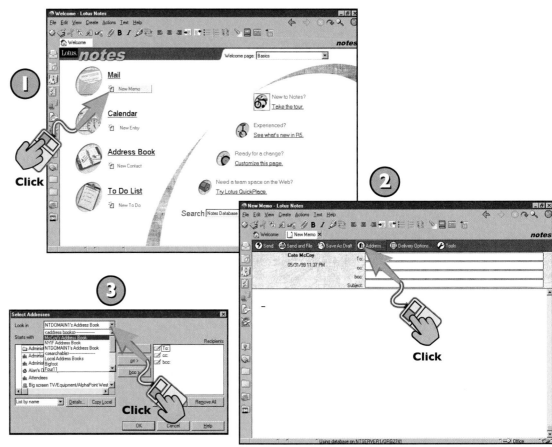

☑ **Group Icon**
The icon for a group is three people huddled together.

☑ **Server Address Book Groups**
Groups in the server's address book can be used in emails, meetings, and To Do tasks. The Domino System Administrator manages these groups.

① Click the **New Memo** button on the Welcome page.

② Click the **Address** button.

③ Click the **Look in** drop-down arrow and select the address book you want to use.

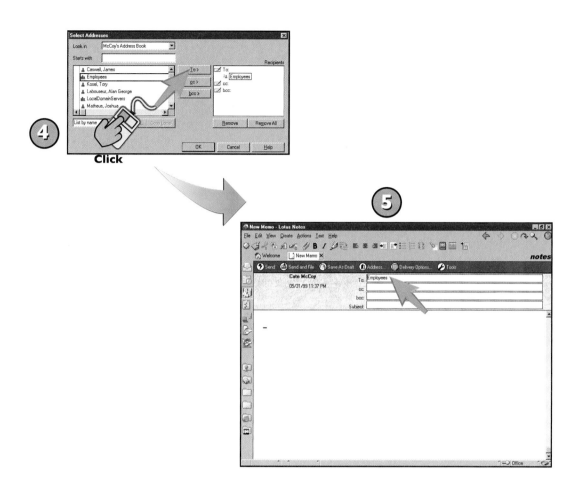

Click

4 Select a group from the list on the left, and click the **To** button to add the group to the email address list on the right. Click **OK** when you finish adding addressees.

5 The Group's name appears in the To field of the message; compose and send the message as normal.

 The Look In Drop-Down List
The address book shown in the **Look in** area defaults to the one most recently used.

End Task

Page
123

Database and Document Basics

Lotus Notes stores its information in *databases*. You can think of a database as a container for information. There are many different databases in Lotus Notes.

Two examples of databases are your mail file and your address book. The mail file is a database that stores information about your incoming and outgoing email. It also stores your calendar and To Do list. The local address book is a separate database that contains information about people and groups with which you frequently interact.

Lotus Notes has many other kinds of databases in addition to the mail file and the address book. In this section, you'll master techniques to effectively apply in any Notes database using a discussion database as an example. A *discussion database* lets many people add their comments on a topic to a database.

Tasks

Databases are located on your local machine or on a Domino server. Your mail file is an example of a database stored on a Domino server. On your local machine, your personal address book is an example of a database stored on your own **PC**. To use the information contained in a database, you need to open it. When you're done with a database, you'll close it.

Task 1: Locating, Opening, and Closing a Database

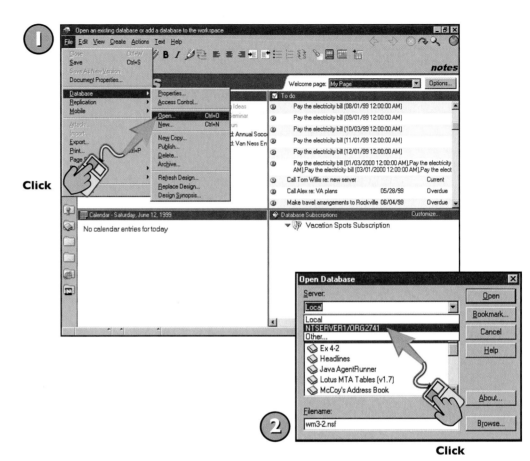

Click

Click

✓ **Domino Servers**
Domino servers have names, like **NTSERVER1/ORG2741**. Your organization may have more than one Domino server, and each one will have a unique name.

✓ **Book Icon**
A blue icon of a book appears to the left of a database. Any of these can be selected and opened.

① Choose **File**, **Database**, **Open**.

② Click the **Server** drop-down arrow and select the location of the database.

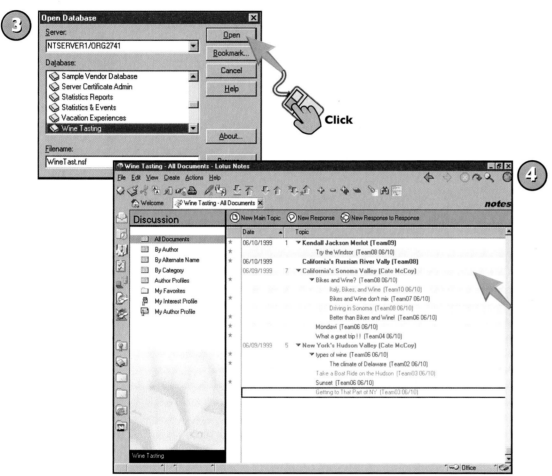

3 Locate a database by scrolling through the **Database** list. Select the database you want, and click the **Open** button.

4 The opened database is displayed and given its own window tab on the Lotus Notes client screen. Click the **Close (X)** button when you're ready to close the database.

✓ Bookmark Button
The **Bookmark** button lets you add the database to one of the bookmarks along the left border of the Notes client without opening the database.

The information in a database is often displayed in two resizable areas on the screen: the Navigator pane and the View pane. The Navigator pane has a list of choices you can click to change the content in the View pane. The View pane contains a list of documents that can be opened.

Task 2: Using the Navigator and View Panes

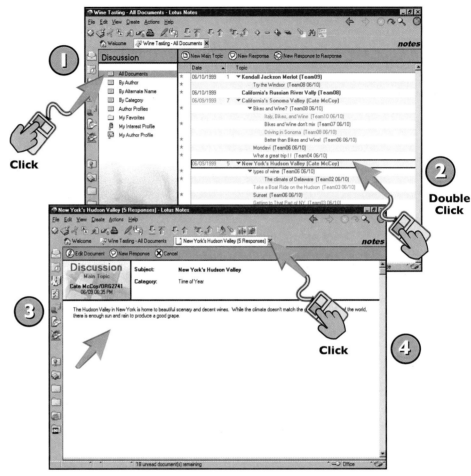

Start Here

Click

①

② **Double Click**

③

Click **④**

✓ Folders

Folders are displayed in the Navigator pane with the icon of a yellow manila folder to the left of the folder name. You can drag and drop documents into the folder.

✓ Unread Marks

The red star in the margin next to a document means that you have not yet opened, or read, this document.

① Click a view name or folder name in the Navigator pane to change the contents of the View pane. In this example, the **All Documents** view is selected, and its documents are displayed in the View pane.

② Double-click a document in the View pane to open it.

③ The contents of the document are displayed.

④ When you finish reading the document, click the **Close (X)** button on the document's window tab.

Next Step

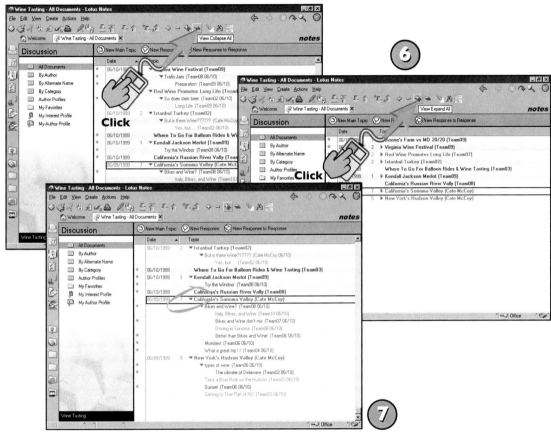

Locate and click the **View Collapse All** SmartIcon to hide documents within a topic category.

The documents are collapsed into categories; the right-pointing triangle in the topic area signals that the category can be expanded. Click the **View Expand All** SmartIcon to redisplay all the documents.

All the documents are once again displayed. The downward-pointing triangle signals that the category is currently expanded.

Response Documents
Documents that are related to a main topic are called *response documents*. A response document is created to respond to the comment in a main topic document. It is indented under the main topic document. A *response to response documents* is created to respond to a comment contained in a response document, and is indented underneath it.

Main Documents
A main topic document in a discussion database creates a new category.

Task 3: Reading and Editing a Document

An open document displays its contents in either read mode or edit mode. Read mode is fine for reading the contents of a document, but to make changes to the content, you must be in edit mode.

✓ Switching to Read Mode
If a document is designed to display in read mode, it will open this way automatically. A document in edit mode can't be switched into read mode.

✓ Rich Text
A rich text typing area lets you format the text by doing things like underlining, bolding, and changing the font color.

✓ Buttons
Some documents have a button bar along the top with buttons to automate certain tasks. If an **Edit Document** button exists, you can click it to open the document instead of double-clicking the document's background.

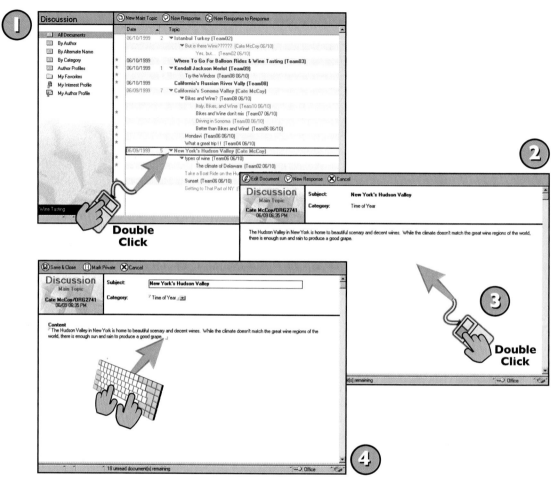

Start Here

Double Click

Double Click

Double-click a document in the View pane to open it.

The document opens in read mode.

Double-click the document's background or use the key combination **Ctrl+E** to put the document in edit mode.

Editable data appears within rectangles or square corner brackets; the square corner brackets are rich-text typing areas. Position your mouse in a typing area, and type away!

End Task

Task 4: Changing Fonts Using the Status Bar

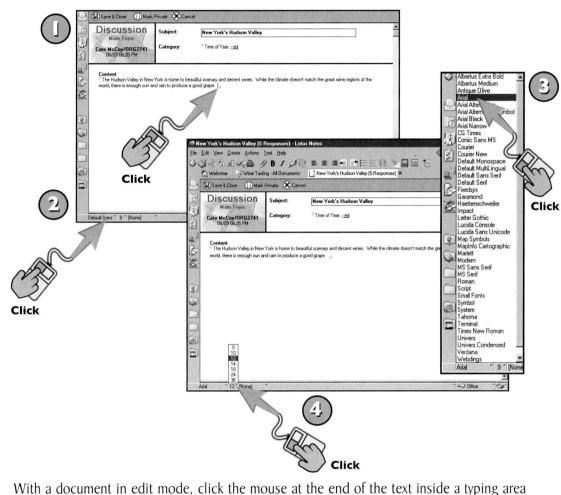

Click (1)

Click (2)

Click (3)

Click (4)

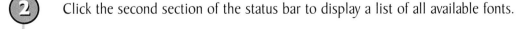

Along the bottom edge of the Lotus Notes client is an eight-section status bar. Each of the clickable sections contains information at different context times within Notes.

✓ **System Messages**
You can see a list of recent system event messages by clicking the large middle section of the status bar.

✓ **Locations**
Locations specify whether your Notes client should talk to a server through a modem connection, an Internet connection, or a local area network connection.

✓ **Typing Areas**
Only typing areas with square corner brackets allow you to change the font.

(1) With a document in edit mode, click the mouse at the end of the text inside a typing area with square corner brackets.

(2) Click the second section of the status bar to display a list of all available fonts.

(3) Click a font to select it.

(4) To change the font size, click the third section of the status bar and select from the pop-up list of sizes that appears. The new font type and size will be used when you continue typing.

Page
131

Task 5: Cutting, Copying, and Pasting Information

The Windows Clipboard can be used to cut, copy, and paste information in Lotus Notes documents. You can copy information from other applications into Notes and vice versa. There are several SmartIcons that will help you quickly perform cut, copy, and paste operations. Although cutting removes the information from the original document, copying leaves the selected information intact.

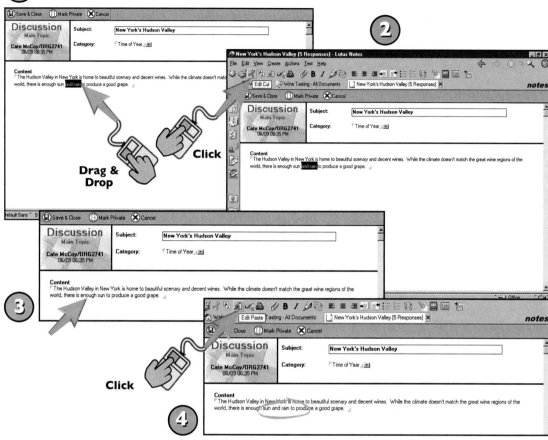

Drag & Drop

Click

Click

✓ **Menu Commands**
After you highlight text, you can use the **Edit** menu to access **Cut, Copy,** and **Paste** options.

✓ **Keyboard Cutting**
Crtl+X cuts highlighted text out of a document.

✓ **Keyboard Pasting**
Crtl+V pastes the contents of the Clipboard into the current document.

 From within a document in edit mode, highlight some text by dragging and dropping the mouse over the text.

 Click the **Edit Cut** SmartIcon to cut the text and place it on the clipboard.

 The information you selected is removed from the document.

 Click the **Edit Paste** SmartIcon to paste the information back in place.

Next Step

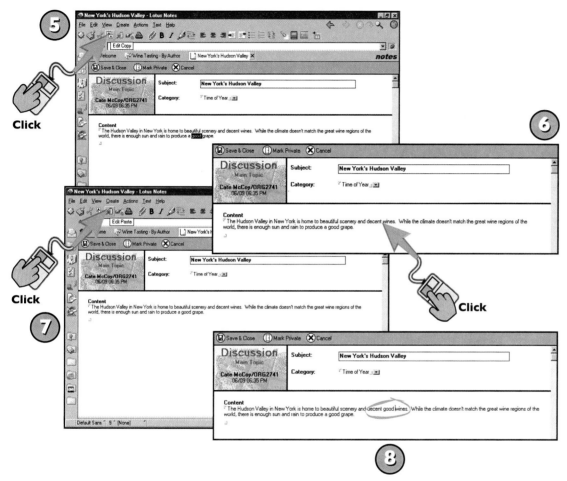

5 To start a copy and paste sequence, highlight a word or phrase, and click the **Edit Copy** SmartIcon to copy the highlighted text to the Clipboard.

6 Click the location in the text where you want the copied information to appear.

7 Click the **Edit Paste** SmartIcon.

8 The text is placed where you clicked.

✓ **Keyboard Copying**
Crtl+C copies highlighted information to the Clipboard.

✓ **Re-pasting**
Information in the Clipboard stays there until it's replaced by the next copy or cut operation, so you can re-paste information.

Task 6: Adding Special Text Effects

Start Here

The **Text** menu provides many special effects—such as bolding, highlighting, spacing, and aligning—that you can apply to text that visually enhance a document. Also, you can associate your favorite font type, size, style, and color with a setting called the *Permanent Pen*. Whenever you enable the Permanent Pen, your settings are used. In editable rich-text typing areas, you have complete control over how the data looks.

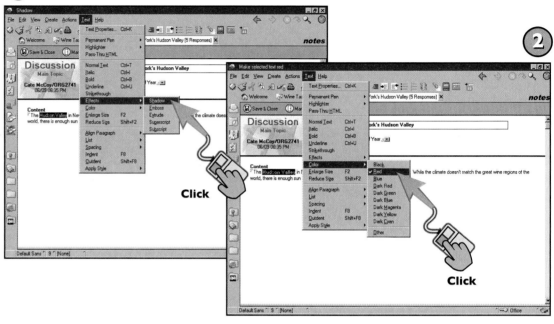

Click

Click

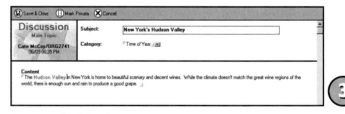

✓ **Highlighted Text**
To apply text effects to existing text, you must first select the text by dragging the mouse across it.

✓ **Edit Mode**
The **Text** menu is only visible on the menu bar when a document is in edit mode.

 With text highlighted in an editable document, choose **Text**, **Effects**, and then select either **Shadow**, **Emboss**, **Extrude**, **Superscript**, or **Subscript** (I chose **Shadow**).

 The effect is applied. With the text still highlighted, choose **Text**, **Color**, and choose a color from the list. (Choosing **Other** lets you choose a color from a drop-down color palette.)

 The color of the text is changed.

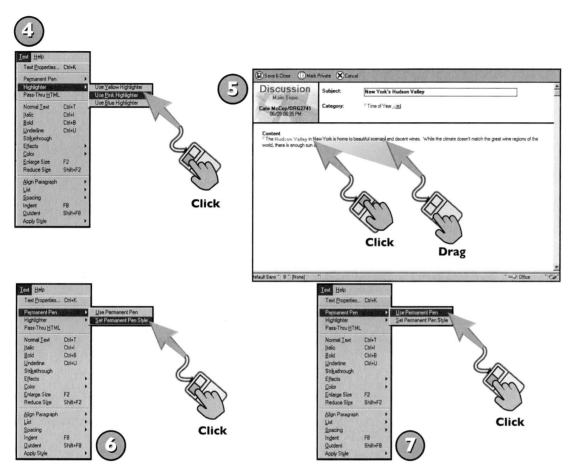

Click

Click **Drag**

Click

Click

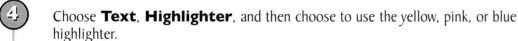

4. Choose **Text**, **Highlighter**, and then choose to use the yellow, pink, or blue highlighter.

5. Using a left-to-right motion, click and drag the mouse pointer over an area of text to highlight it with the see-through color.

6. Choose **Text**, **Permanent Pen**, **Set Permanent Pen Style**. This establishes the current font style, color, and size as the Permanent Pen settings.

7. To use the Permanent Pen settings when you type, choose **Text**, **Permanent Pen**, **Use Permanent Pen**; then type away!

✅ **Permanent Pen**
Using the Permanent Pen is a good way to quickly switch to a font style that you use on a regular basis. The default font color is red.

✅ **Context Menus**
Clicking the right mouse button over selected text opens a context menu to provide quick access to many of the special text effects.

End Task

Task 7: Building Lists in a Document

Itemized lists are a great way to concisely present information. You can create a variety of lists to itemize content in a rich-text typing area in a document. Lotus Notes contains several list styles to choose from including bullet, number, check mark, circle, square, uppercase alphabetic, lowercase alphabetic, uppercase Roman numerals, or lowercase Roman numerals.

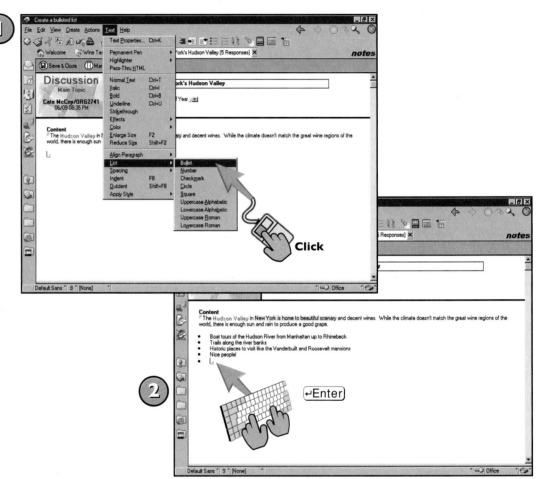

✓ **Adding Bullets After the Fact**

To itemize text after it's already created, select the text, and choose **Text, List.** Then choose one of the list styles.

✓ **Currently Selected Style**

If a style is currently in effect, a check mark appears to the left of the style name in the **List** menu.

① In a rich-text area of a document in edit mode, choose **Text**, **List**, and choose one of the Lotus Notes list styles.

② As you type text in the typing area, you can press the **Enter** key to create a new line break, and thus create a new list item.

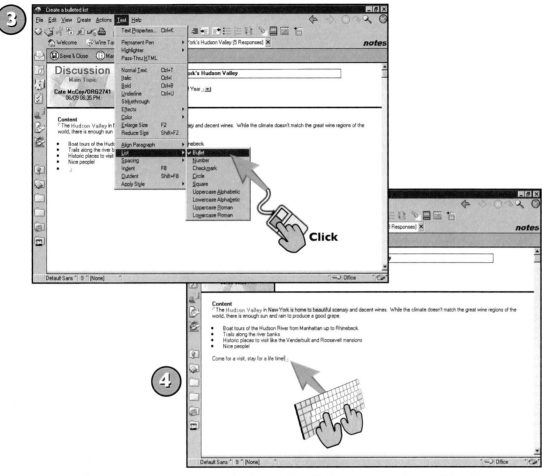

To stop typing list items, you must turn the list style off. Once again, choose **Text**, **List**, and click the list style to remove the check mark.

When you begin typing again, the list style is no longer in effect.

Task 8: Working with Tables

Tables are useful for organizing information and aligning blocks of data in documents that you create. Basic tables consist of rows and columns, and are useful in adding borders around important information. Tables can be added to any rich-text typing area.

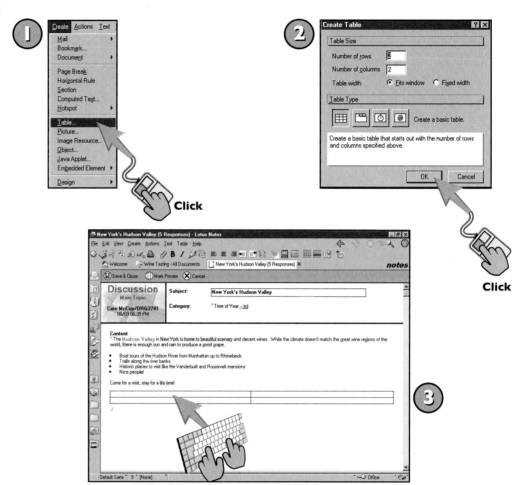

Click

Click

✓ **Fixed-Width Tables**
To set a table at a specific width regardless of the size of the computer screen, select the **Fixed width** radio button in the Create Table dialog box.

✓ **Nested Tables**
You can create a table within a cell of another table.

1 Choose **Create**, **Table...**.

2 The Create Table dialog box defaults to creating a table with two rows and two columns that fits the window; you can change the table size to fit your needs. Click the **OK** button to create the table.

3 A table with cells is added to the typing area. To type information in a cell in the table, just click in the cell and start typing!

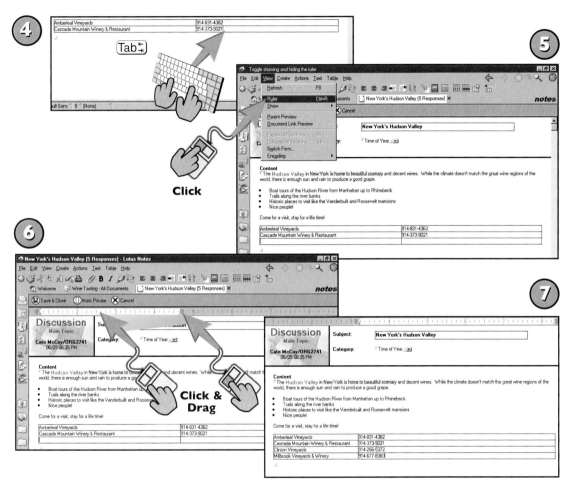

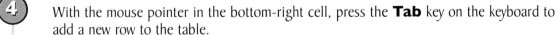

(4) With the mouse pointer in the bottom-right cell, press the **Tab** key on the keyboard to add a new row to the table.

(5) To resize the columns in the table, begin by choosing **View**, **Ruler**.

(6) Cell borders are represented on the ruler by gray squares. Drag the squares left or right to change the width of the selected column.

(7) The column is resized.

✓ **Cell Margins**
Each cell has a margin, which determines how closely the text is aligned against the cell border. Cell margins are represented on the ruler by a top-pointing triangle. Change the cell margin by dragging and dropping the triangle to the left or the right.

✓ **Aligning Column Text**
Align the text within a column by selecting the column, and then choosing **Text, Align Paragraph**.

✓ **Advanced Table Options**
The Create Table dialog box lets you create tabbed tables, animated tables, and programmed tables by clicking a different **Table Type** button.

A rich-text typing area can contain many different kinds of information including text, tables, audio files, video files, and spreadsheets. You can create attachments to any Notes document using any type of external data. This task demonstrates attaching an Excel spreadsheet to a Discussion Database document.

Task 9: Attaching a Microsoft Excel Spreadsheet

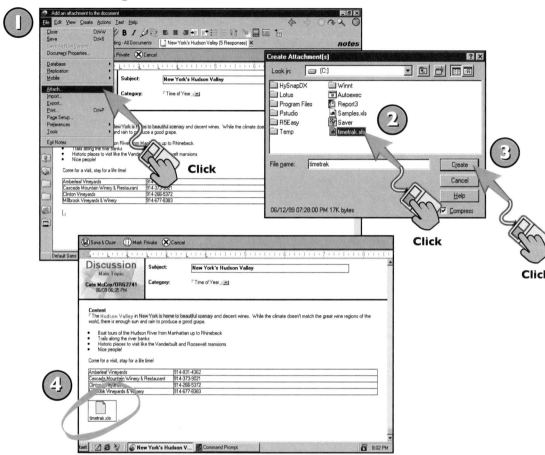

In a rich-text typing area, choose **File**, **Attach**.

In the **Create Attachment(s)** dialog box, locate the file you want to attach, and then click it to select it.

Click the **Create** button to create an attachment to the current document.

The document is added as an attachment.

Task 10: Saving and Closing Documents

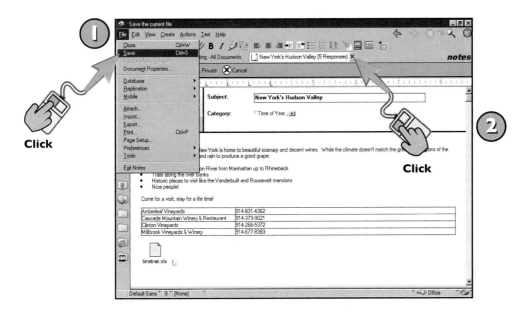

Click

Click

Click

After you edit a document, you can save it to make your changes permanent. You can save the document without closing it or you can save it as you exit from it.

① To save a document without closing it, choose **File**, **Save**. You can continue editing the document, saving the information as frequently as you feel is necessary.

② To save and then exit a document, click the **Close (X)** button on the document's window tab.

③ If the document is in edit mode and changes have been made since the last time you saved it, you are asked if you want to save your changes. Click **Yes** to save the changes and exit the document.

✓ **Saving Using the Keyboard**
Save a document without exiting by pressing the **Ctrl+S** key combination on the keyboard.

✓ **The Esc Key**
Pressing the **Esc** key on the keyboard closes the current document.

Task 11: Deleting Documents

Deleting documents is a two-step process. First, you mark the document for deletion using the **Delete** key. Second, you "empty the trash" by refreshing or closing the database.

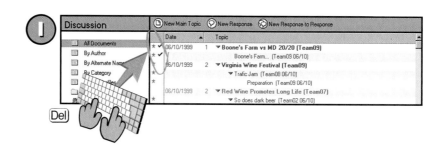

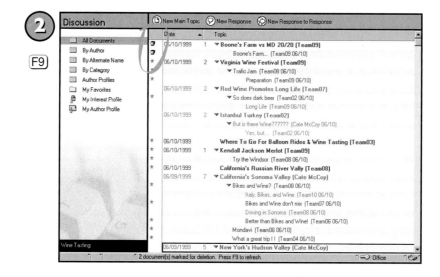

Change Your Mind?
To remove the trash can icon and unmark the document, press the **Delete** key again. The **Delete** key works like an on/off switch.

Refreshing the Database
Refreshing rereads the contents of what is physically stored on the hard drive for the database and rewrites the updated information to the screen.

Menu Options
Choosing **View, Refresh** is the same as pressing the **F9** key.

1 Select a document (or multiple documents) in a view, and press the **Delete** key on the keyboard to mark the documents for deletion.

2 The trash can icon appears in the margin area next to the document, which marks the document for deletion. Press the **F9** key on the keyboard to throw the marked documents away.

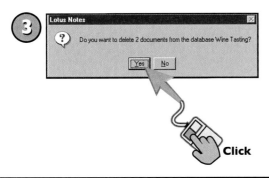

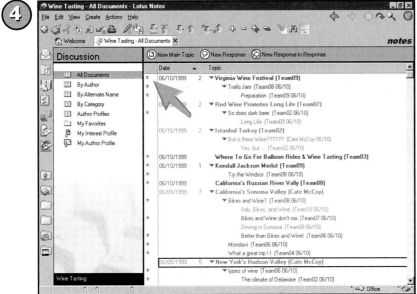

③ A message appears asking you if you're sure you want to delete the documents. Click **Yes** to complete the document-deletion process.

④ The documents are deleted.

Task 12: Printing Documents

The contents of a document can be printed while the document is open or when it is listed in the View pane. From the View pane, you can select multiple documents to send to the printer.

Start Here

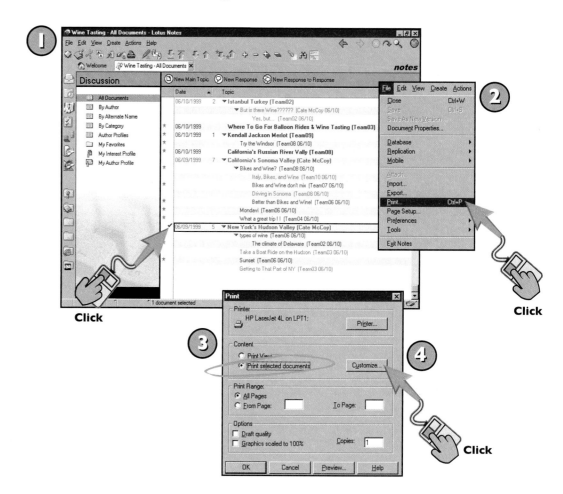

Click

Click

Click

✅ **Fast Document Selection**
To select multiple documents that are listed together, drag the mouse pointer over the documents in the margin area and release it when all the documents you want to print are selected.

✅ **Deselecting a Document**
Click the check mark for a selected document to deselect it. To deselect a group of selected documents, drag the mouse pointer in the margin area.

① Click the margin area to the left of a document's subject text. A check mark appears, signaling that the document has been selected.

② Choose **File**, **Print**.

✅ **Printing the Displayed Document**
To print a document that is open on the screen, choose **File, Print**.

③ The **Content** option button defaults to **Print selected documents** (those with check marks in the margin area or the document you were viewing when you chose **File**, **Print**).

④ Click the **Customize...** button.

Next Step

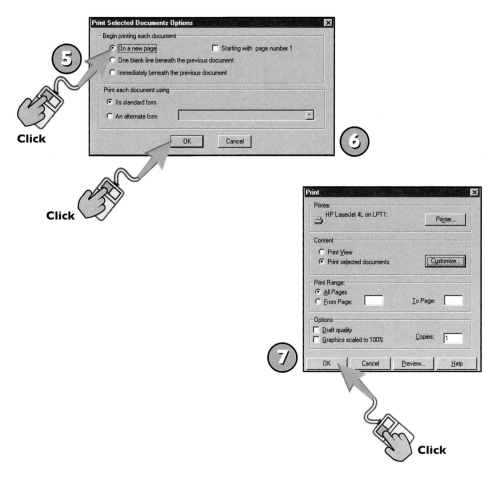

5 Select an option button to separate multiple documents with either a page break, a blank line, or no separator at all.

6 Click the **OK** button to save your customizations.

7 Click the **OK** button to send the document(s) to the printer.

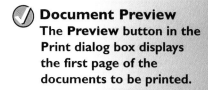

Document Preview
The **Preview** button in the Print dialog box displays the first page of the documents to be printed.

Task 13: Printing a View List

The **Print** dialog box lets you customize what page (or pages) is printed, the number of copies that are printed, and which printer the documents are sent to.

✓ **Printer Setup**
The available printers are determined by Windows, not by Lotus Notes. To add a printer, click the **Start** button on the Windows desktop, choose **Settings**, select **Printers**, and double-click the **Add Printer** icon. Then follow the steps in the wizard to add the printer you need.

✓ **Number of Copies**
The default number of copies printed is one. Change this as necessary in the **Copies** area of the Print dialog box.

✓ **Print Range**
For views that contain many documents, use the **Print Range** option to specify whether to print all the pages or to specify a starting and ending page number.

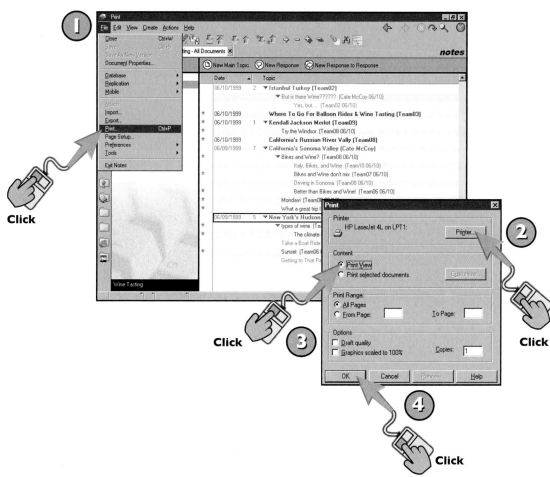

Click

Click

Click

Click

1. With a list of documents in the View pane, choose **File**, **Print...**.

2. Confirm that the active printer is the one you want, or click the **Printer** button to change it.

3. Click the **Print View** option button.

4. Click the **OK** button to send the list of documents shown in the **View** to the printer. This prints the list of documents as they appear on the View screen, not the contents of the documents.

Task 14: Enabling Subscription Services

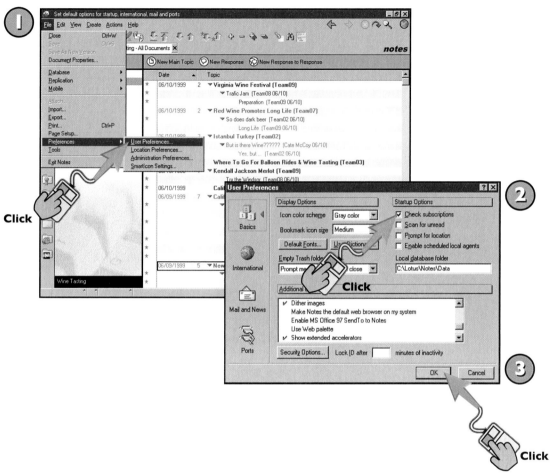

Click

Click

Click

Notes can automatically notify you when information is added to certain types of Notes databases, like discussion databases. You can subscribe to receive updates after you enable subscription monitoring in your Notes client. When a change is detected, a notification is added to the **Database Subscriptions** area of a customized **Welcome** page. You need to enable your Notes client to check for subscription updates.

① From any place in Notes, choose **File**, **Preferences**, **User Preferences...**.

② In the Startup Options area of the User Preferences dialog box, click the **Check subscriptions** option to turn on subscription monitoring.

③ Click the **OK** button to save your change and enable subscription monitoring.

✓ **Displaying Subscription Notices**
The "Customizing Your Welcome Page" task in Part 1, "Welcome Page Basics," shows you how to modify the Welcome page. In the **Options** area, you can select **Database Subscriptions** as a type of frame content.

If a database can be subscribed to, it contains a **Subscriptions** option in its **Create** menu. To create a subscription profile, you must be inside the database you want to subscribe to.

Task 15: Subscribing to Database Updates

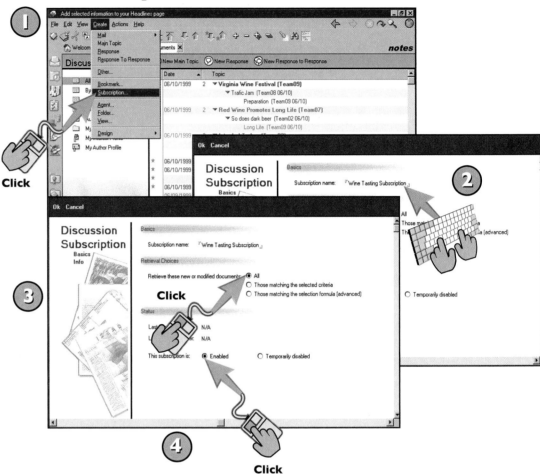

Start Here

Click

Click

Click

Click

(✓) **Document Selection Criteria**
The **Retrieve Documents** check boxes can be used to select only documents that reference a specific author, subject, category, or thread activity. More than one of these options can be chosen at one time.

(1) From within a database that supports subscriptions, like a discussion database, choose **Create**, **Subscription...**.

(2) A Discussion Subscription application form is displayed. Type a brief and meaningful name to describe the subscription in the **Subscription name** field in the **Basics** area.

(3) Click an option button to specify whether you want to receive all updates or only updates matching certain criteria.

(4) Start the subscription monitoring process by clicking the **Enabled** option button.

Next Step

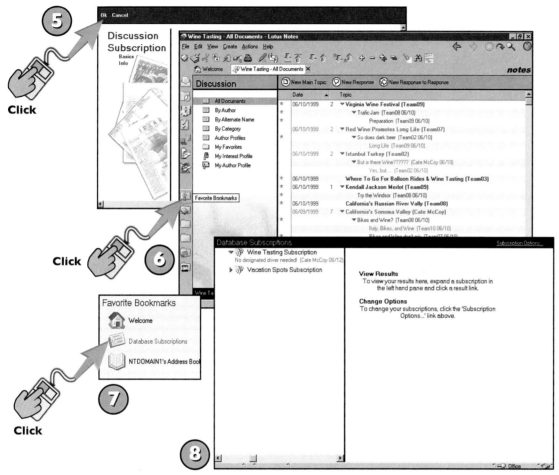

5 Click the **Ok** button to close the Subscription Application form.

6 Click the **Favorite Bookmarks** on the left border of the Notes window.

7 Click the **Database Subscriptions** link to open the database and verify that the new subscription has been added.

8 The left side of the screen shows the title of the database you've subscribed to, and all notifications you've received for the database.

Task 16: Maintaining Your Subscriptions

Subscription notifications for all databases are automatically sent to the database subscriptions database. That way, you need only check one place for information about changes in any of the databases to which you've subscribed. You can make changes to the subscription at any time if you want to receive less or more information or cancel the entire subscription.

✅ **Welcome Page**
For easy access to database updates, customize your Welcome page to add database subscriptions as one of the content frames. Refer to Task 4, "Customizing Your Welcome Page" in Part 1 of this book to learn how to customize your Welcome page.

✅ **Subscription Results**
The window tab for the database subscriptions link is labeled **Subscription Results**.

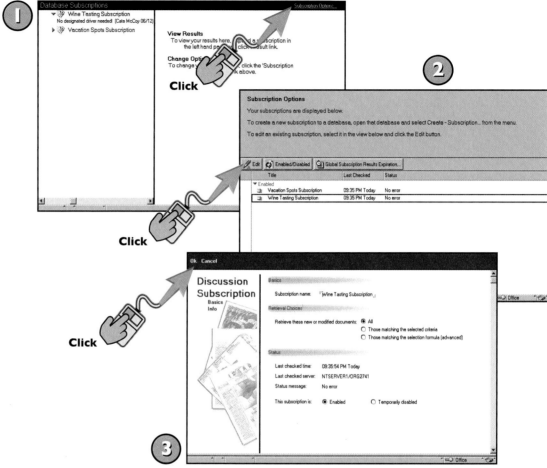

Click

Click

Click

With the database subscriptions database open, click the **Subscription Options...** link near the top-right corner.

Select a subscription from the list and click the **Edit** button.

The subscription information is displayed. After making any changes, click the **Ok** button to save the subscription settings.

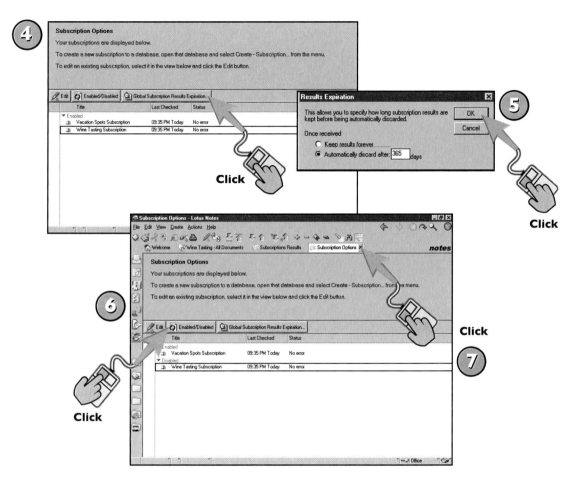

Enabled Subscriptions
Subscriptions that are currently being monitored display in the **Enabled** category.

Disabled Subscriptions
A subscription that has been disabled using the **Enabled/Disabled** button displays in the **Disabled** category.

Canceling a Subscription
You can terminate subscription services on a database by selecting the subscription in the list and pressing the **Delete** key and then pressing the **F9** key to refresh the screen.

(4) Click the **Global Subscription Results Expiration** button to examine how long each subscription notification will be kept.

(5) The default subscription saves notification messages for a year unless you delete them sooner. Click the **OK** button to save any changes.

(6) Click the **Enabled/Disabled** button to change the current monitoring status from enabled to disabled or vice versa.

(7) Close the **Subscription Options** area by clicking the **Close (X)** button on its window tab.

Take Your Notes R5 Client on the Road

The Lotus Notes R5 client can be used in standalone mode to process information stored on your PC, or it can be used with a Domino server to process information on a server that is shared by many users.

While you're traveling across the country in Seat 22A at 35,000 feet, you can be working on mail that you downloaded before you left the office. At home or from a hotel room on the road, you can use a modem connection between your PC and the Domino server to upload your changes. Notes uses a set of documents called *location documents* to keep track of where you are when you're working on Notes so that it can process uploads and downloads efficiently. The process of uploading and downloading changes is called *replication* in Notes.

This section shows you how to replicate databases, change locations, and configure connections so that you can go mobile with Notes.

Tasks

Task 1: Preparing to Work Offline

To work in standalone mode, you create a copy of a database on the server and store it on your PC. This is known as making a *replica copy* of a database. Replica copies of a database share information between one another when you decide to upload or download changes. This example shows how to make a replica copy of a discussion database so that you can read updates offline or create new documents remotely.

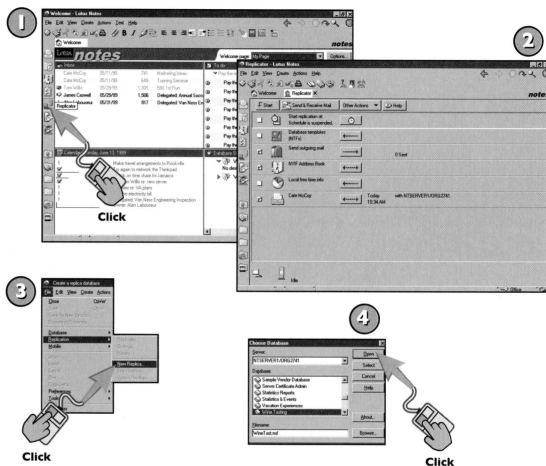

Click

Click

Click

✓ **Replicator Databases**
The Replicator window lists the databases that currently have replica copies on your PC.

✓ **Choosing a Database**
You can bypass the Choose Database dialog box if you choose **File, Replication, New Replica** from within a database you want a copy of; Notes assumes the current database is your choice.

Locate and click the **Replicator** bookmark along the left side of the Lotus Notes screen.

The Replicator page is displayed.

Choose **File**, **Replication**, **New Replica**.

The Choose Database dialog box opens. Choose the server that houses the database you want to make a replica of, choose the database itself, and click the **Open** button.

Next Step

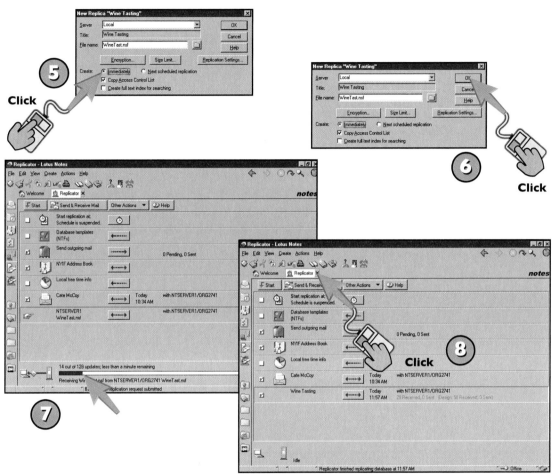

Click

Click

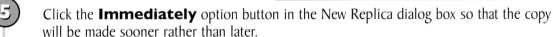

Click

⑤ Click the **Immediately** option button in the New Replica dialog box so that the copy will be made sooner rather than later.

⑥ The defaults are set to make a replica copy of the database and store it on your local PC. Click the **OK** button to create the replica copy.

⑦ As the replica copy is being made, progress information is displayed on the bottom of the Replicator window.

⑧ When the process is complete, the status bar reports that the database has been replicated. Close the Replicator window by clicking the **Close (X)** button on its window tab.

✔ **Local Server**
Notes uses the term *local* to refer to information stored on your PC. Because your PC is serving up information, it is considered a *local server*. It is not, however, a Domino server.

✔ **Next Scheduled Replication**
A Domino server replicates (uploads and downloads) information on a schedule put in place by the System Administrator.

✔ **Replication Summary**
The database is listed on the Replicator window with a summary of how many documents were received and sent.

End Task

Task 2: Working in a Database Replica

A replica database looks exactly like its original, and you process information in the replica in the same ways you would in the original—which can generate a bit of confusion sometimes! It's a good idea to create a bookmark for your replica databases so that you always know whether you're working with the replica or the original.

Start Here

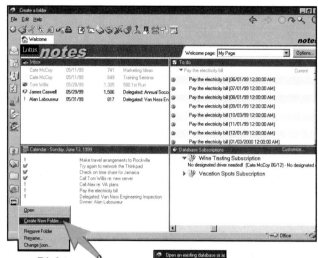

Right-Click

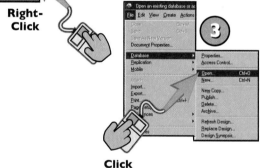

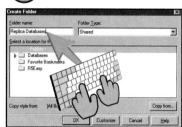

Click

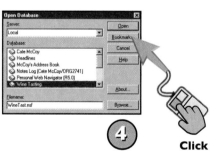

Click

 Folder Names and Icons

You can rename the folder or change its icon by right-clicking it and selecting the **Rename** and **Change Icon** options.

① Right-click an open area on the bookmark bar and choose the **Create New Folder** option.

② Type **Replica Databases** as the name of the folder, and then click **OK**.

③ Add a database to the new bookmark by choosing **File**, **Database**, **Open**.

④ Locate the local replica copy of a database, select it, and click the **Bookmark** button.

Next Step

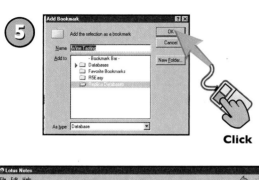

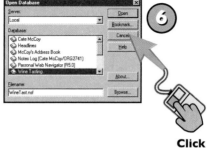

Click

Click

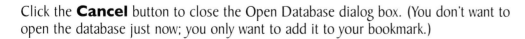

Click

(7)

(8)

5 The Add Bookmark dialog box opens. Select the bookmark to which you want to add the replica database, and then click the **OK** button.

6 Click the **Cancel** button to close the Open Database dialog box. (You don't want to open the database just now; you only want to add it to your bookmark.)

7 Click the new **Replica Databases** bookmark to open it.

8 The bookmark expands, showing that the database has been added. From here, you can open the database to work with it.

End Task

✓ **Tacking a Bookmark Open**
At the top-left corner of an open bookmark panel, a square icon with three horizontal lines can be used to pin a bookmark window open. That way, it won't automatically slide closed.

After reading documents and updating information in your replica copy of a database, you'll want to synchronize the changes with the original database. This process is called *replication.* You can send your changes to the original database, receive changes that were made to the original database, or do both at the same time.

✓ **Blue Arrow Pointing Left**
Changes in the server database will be received (downloaded) and added to the local database.

✓ **Blue Arrow Pointing Right**
Changes in the local database will be sent (uploaded) to the server database.

✓ **Blue Arrow Pointing Both Ways**
Changes will be sent to and received from the server. This is an upload to the server and a download from the server.

Task 3: Replicating Changes Between Servers

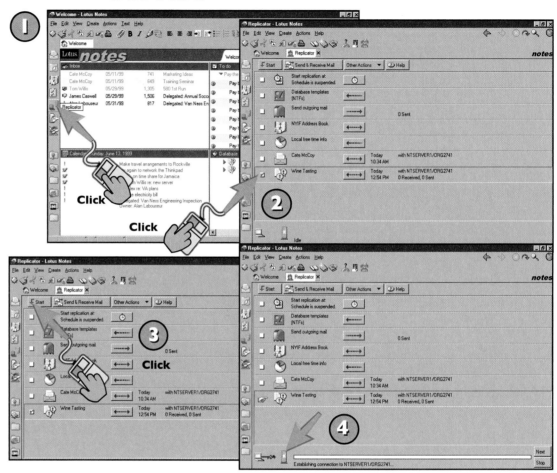

(1) Click the **Replicator** bookmark along the left edge of the Lotus Notes screen.

(2) Click the white square to the left of the database you want to replicate to make it active.

(3) Click the **Start** button to replicate changes for the databases marked with a check.

(4) The changes are exchanged. You can watch the progress on the bottom of the Replicator page; it will return to Idle when it's done.

Task 4: Changing Your Notes Client Location

Start Here

 1

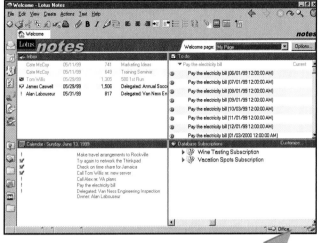

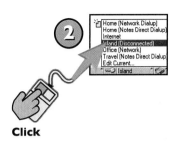 **2**

Click

Click

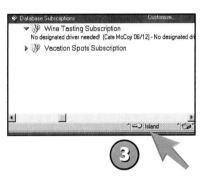

3

Your Lotus Notes client contains settings that allow it to communicate with the outside world. These settings are stored in a location document. To work with Notes outside of your office, you need to change your location so that Notes can figure out how to connect to remote servers.

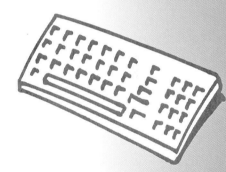

1 Your current location is listed on the status bar of the Lotus Notes screen, in the Location (second-to-last) section. Click the **Location** section to display your options.

2 Switch to a different location by clicking a choice in the list.

3 The location information on the status bar changes.

✓ **Keyboard Access**
To change locations using the keyboard, choose **File, Mobile, Choose Current Location.**

End Task

Task 5: Opening and Editing Location Documents

Location documents are stored in your local personal address book. Notes automatically created several location documents for you, and you can create additional ones to customize access for specialized communication.

✅ **Home (Network Dial-Up)**
Use this location to dial into your company's Domino server using TCP/IP dial-in software provided by your company.

✅ **Home (Notes Direct Dial-Up)**
Use this location to dial the phone number of a Domino server directly using a communications port.

✅ **Internet**
Use this location to connect to the Internet using TCP/IP.

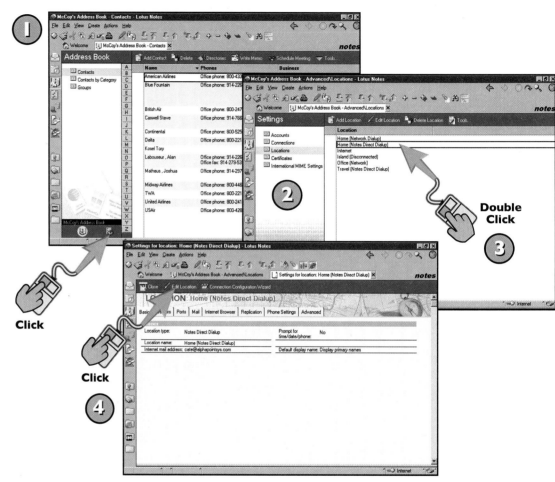

From within your personal address book, click the **Advanced Settings** icon in the lower-right corner of the Navigator pane.

The **Settings** window contains a list of advanced areas. With the **Locations** option selected, the existing location documents are listed in the View pane.

Double-click a location document to open it.

Click the **Edit Location** button to put the location document into edit mode.

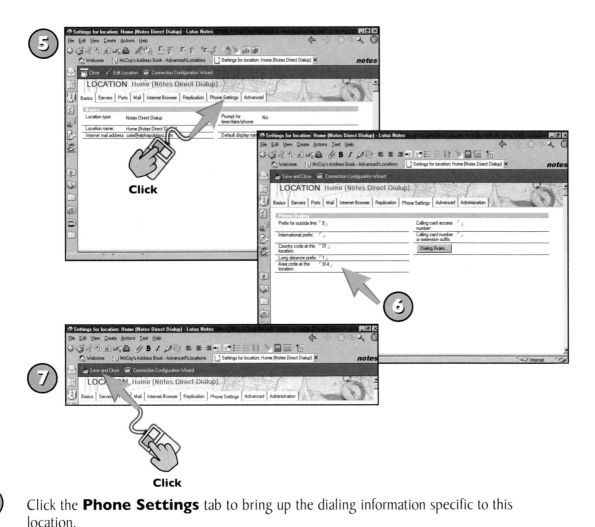

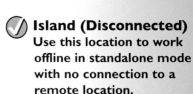

(5) Click the **Phone Settings** tab to bring up the dialing information specific to this location.

(6) Record information on this tab to tell the Notes client how to dial an outside line.

(7) Click the **Save and Close** button to save your changes.

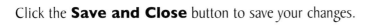

✔ **Island (Disconnected)**
Use this location to work offline in standalone mode with no connection to a remote location.

✔ **Office (Network)**
Use this location when connected to a Domino server through a local area network.

✔ **Travel (Notes Direct Dial-Up)**
Use this location when using a modem to dial in from hotels.

End Task

Task 6: Enabling Communications Ports for Remote Access

Communications ports are used by your computer to physically connect to other computers. In the office, this is often through a network card and cable using a TCP/IP port. TCP/IP is also the port used to access the Internet. On the road, a computer modem and a phone line can connect to a Domino server using a communications port, which is commonly called a **COM** port. To dial into a Domino server with a modem, you need to enable the COM ports in your Lotus Notes client.

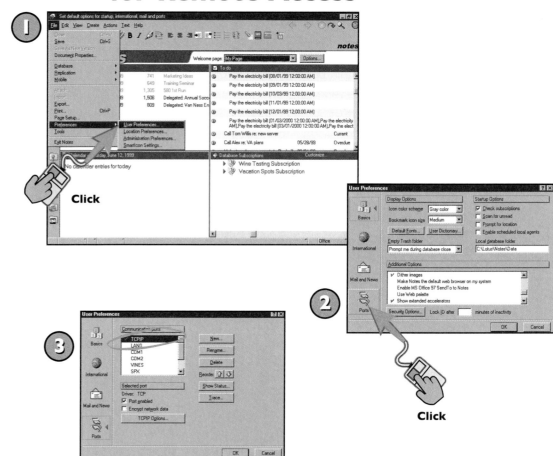

Click

Click

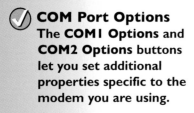 **COM Port Options**
The **COM1 Options** and **COM2 Options** buttons let you set additional properties specific to the modem you are using.

 Choose **File**, **Preferences**, **User Preferences**.

 Click the **Ports** button on the left side of the User Preferences dialog box.

 The available communications ports are listed, with the ones that are active noted with a check mark. In this example, only the TCP/IP protocol is active.

Next Step

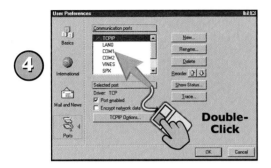

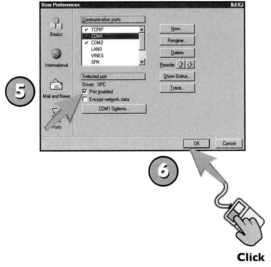

Double-Click

Click

④ Double-click the **COM1** and **COM2** options to enable modem communications on both of these ports.

⑤ The **Port enabled** check box is checked for the active communications ports, and a check mark appears alongside the port name in the list.

⑥ Click the **OK** button to save your communication port changes.

Reordering Ports
When Notes tries to connect to a Domino server, it starts at the top of the list of enabled ports. You can change the order of the ports using the **Reorder** up and down arrows to move the port you most frequently use to the top of the list.

Before you can use a modem to talk to a Domino server, you need to tell Lotus Notes which modem you're using and configure options to make it efficient. These settings are configured in the Ports User Preferences options.

Task 7: Configuring Notes to Use a Modem

 Start Here

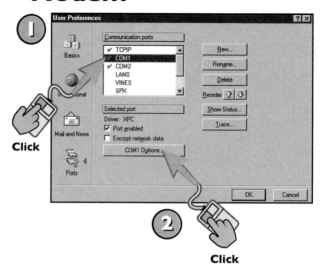

Click

② Click

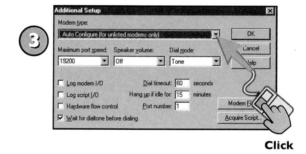

③

Click

✓ **Your Modem Isn't Listed?**

If your modem isn't in the drop-down list of modem types, try using the **Auto Configure** option. You can also check your modem's documentation for tips and suggestions, or seek out help desk support.

① From the User Preferences dialog box, click on a **COM** port to select it. (If you need help accessing this dialog box, refer to the preceding task.)

② Click the **Options** button. (The label on this button changes depending on which port is selected. For instance, if **COM1** is selected, the button will be labeled **COM1 Options**.)

③ Click the **Modem type** drop-down arrow, and locate and select the one being used in your PC.

 Next Step

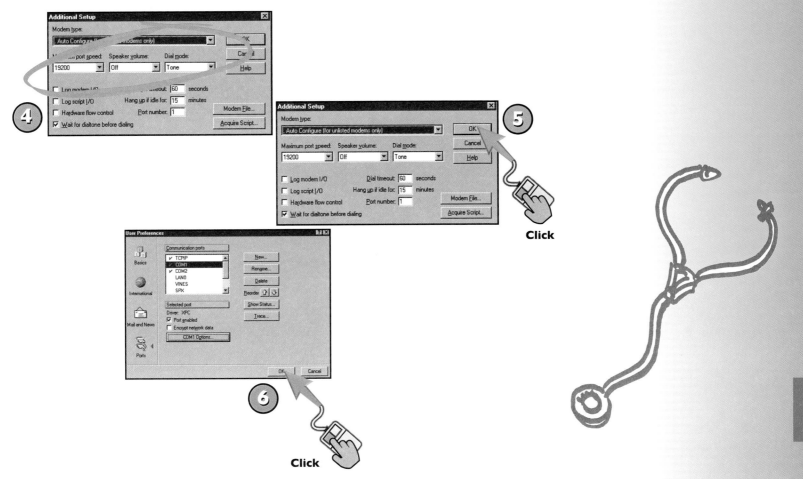

Click

Click

④ Set or verify the options for maximum port speed and dial mode (check your modem's documentation), and speaker volume.

⑤ Click the **OK** button to save the modem settings.

⑥ Click **OK** again to save and exit the User Preferences screen. Your modem is now configured to work with Notes.

End Task

Task 8: Making a Connection to a Remote Server

Notes uses *connection documents* to configure settings to work with remote servers. Like location documents, connection documents are stored in your personal name and address book. The easiest way to create a new connection document is to use the Connection Configuration Wizard while you're editing a location document.

✓ **Passthru Server**
A passthru server lets you connect to multiple servers using one connection document. You can set up a passthru server to be a default if your regular connection fails.

Start Here

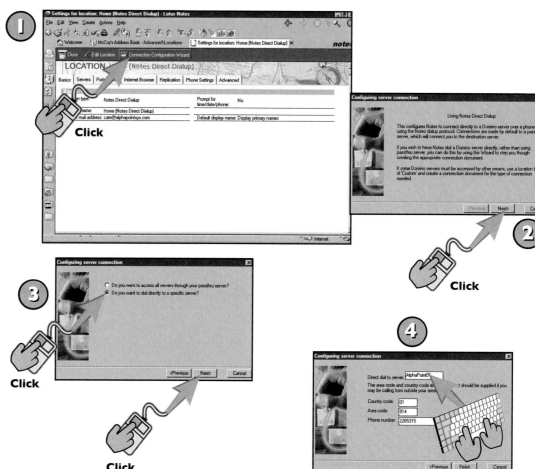

Click

Click

Click

Click

1 From within a location document, click the **Connection Configuration Wizard** button.

2 The wizard opens, and presents the first screen to walk you through configuring a connection. Click the **Next** button.

3 Select the option button that describes the kind of connection you are making. (In this example, a direct dial connection is being configured.) Click **Next**.

4 Type the name of the destination server, the server's country code, its area code, and its phone number. (You'll probably need to ask your System Administrator for this information.)

Next Step

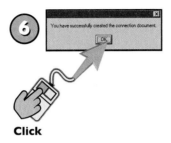

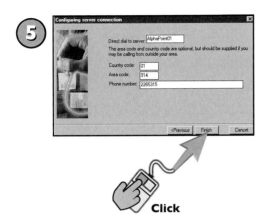

Click

Click

Click

Click

(5) Click the **Finish** button to save the settings.

(6) Click the **OK** button on the confirmation dialog box.

(7) Click the **Save and Close** button to exit the location document.

(8) To see where your new connection document was stored, click the **Connections** option in the Navigator pane, which lists the documents in the View pane.

✓ **Location Documents**
If you use a passthru server, add the server name to the location document. This allows it to use the passthru connection document.

End Task

Task 9: Sending and Receiving Mail Remotely

When you are not working with a Domino server interactively, Notes automatically creates an outgoing mailbox with an icon on the Replicator page. You work in your mail file as you normally would, and then use the Replicator page to send the outgoing mail when you're ready.

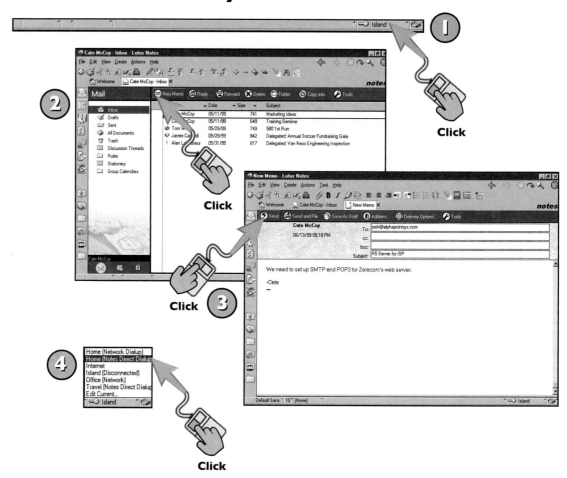

✓ **Send & Receive Mail**
The **Send & Receive Mail** button exchanges mail between all mail databases, not just the ones that have a check mark. However, only those valid for the current location will succeed.

Start Here

1 Select the **Island** location document by clicking the **Location** area of the status bar and selecting **Island**.

2 Click the **New Memo** button to write a new memo.

3 Address and write the memo as you normally would, then click the **Send** button. The memo is closed and stored in an outgoing mailbox.

4 To send the mail, click the **Location** area in the status bar and select a location that has a dial-in configuration—for example, **Home (Notes Direct Dialup)**.

Next Step

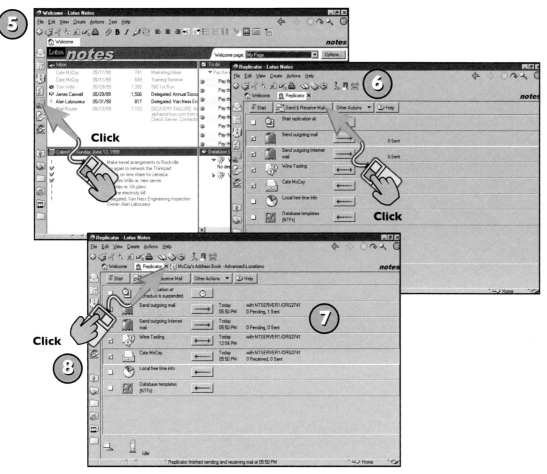

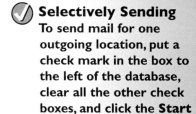

5 Click the **Replicator** bookmark to open the Replicator page.

6 Click the **Send & Receive Mail** button on the top of the Replicator page. The Replicator uses the information in your location and connection documents to call a server.

7 The Replicator processes the mail, and reports the status of how many were sent and received.

8 Click the **Close (X)** button to exit from the Replicator page.

Selectively Sending
To send mail for one outgoing location, put a check mark in the box to the left of the database, clear all the other check boxes, and click the **Start** button.

End Task

Internet Access
with Notes R5

The information on the Internet has become critical to our success in a knowledge-intensive work environment. The goal of the R5 interface is quick access to everything, from your Notes mail, to Web sites, to Internet newsgroups, and everything in between. This section shows you how to configure Notes to use the Internet as a key piece in solving the knowledge management puzzle.

Tasks

Task 1: Adding the Web to Your Welcome Page

If you have a live connection to the Internet in your office environment or via an Internet service provider (ISP), you can add the Web to your Welcome page. Customizing the frame content lets Notes connect to your favorite Web page each time you open the Notes client.

✓ **Dial-Up Networking**
For information on how to configure dial-up networking for a Windows-based system, search the help file in Windows 95, Window 98, or Windows NT.

✓ **Web Page Address**
Selecting the option to type an address lets you enter any valid Uniform Resource Locator (URL) address including the http:// prefix.

✓ **Locations**
With a live Internet connection, you can display a Web page in the Welcome page using all Location documents.

Start Here

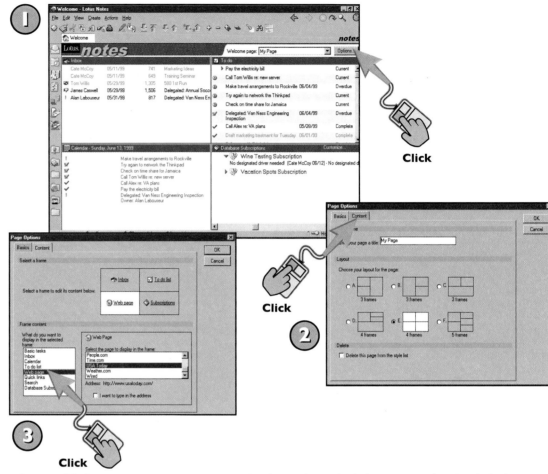

Click

Click

Click

① After establishing an Internet connection (perhaps through dial-up networking), click the **Options...** button to modify your custom Welcome page.

② Click the **Content** tab.

③ In the Frame content area at the bottom of the window, select the **Web page** option.

Next Step

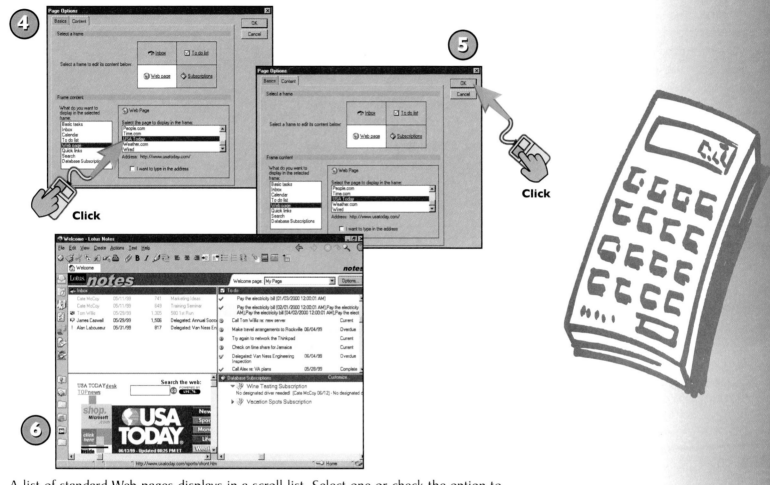

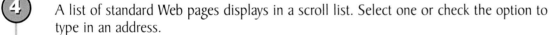

<table>
</table>

4. A list of standard Web pages displays in a scroll list. Select one or check the option to type in an address.

5. Click the **OK** button to save your changes.

6. Your custom Welcome page now displays the Web page you selected.

Task 2: Choosing a Web Browser for a Location

The settings in your Internet location document determine how you access the Internet when you don't already have an active connection to it. In addition to Internet Explorer (IE) and Netscape Navigator, Notes has a built-in Web browser called the *Personal Web Navigator*.

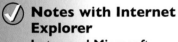

Click

Click

Click

✓ **Notes with Internet Explorer**
Lotus and Microsoft teamed up to create an Internet Explorer (IE) browser internal to the Notes environment.

✓ **Notes Personal Web Browser**
The Notes browser offers the tightest integration with the rest of the Lotus Notes client, and has features like page caching and offline browsing.

1 Click the **Location** area of the status bar, and select the **Internet** option.

2 Click the **Location** area of the status bar again; this time choose the **Edit Current...** option.

3 Click the **Internet Browser** tab.

Next Step

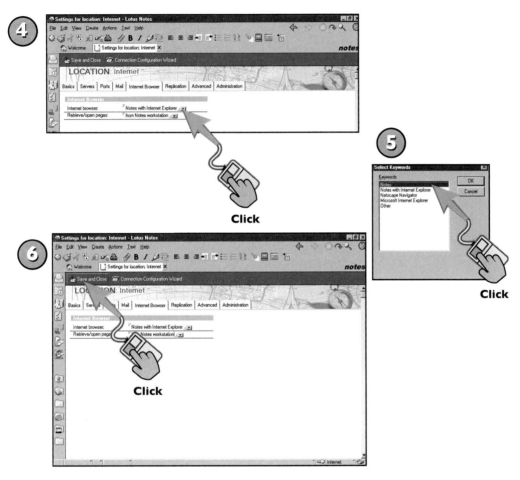

Click

Click

Click

④ Click the drop-down arrow to display the Internet browser choices.

⑤ Set a default browser by selecting one from the list (for the sake of example, select the **Notes** option to use the Notes Personal Web Navigator) and clicking the **OK** button.

⑥ Save your changes by clicking the **Save and Close** button.

The Personal Web Navigator is a Notes database, so all you already know about Notes databases can be used in this browser as well. If your organization has standardized on the Notes browser, it's because it reduces the learning curve, limits problems related to external Web browser support, and offers advanced features for working offline in the Notes environment.

Task 3: Using the Notes Personal Web Navigator

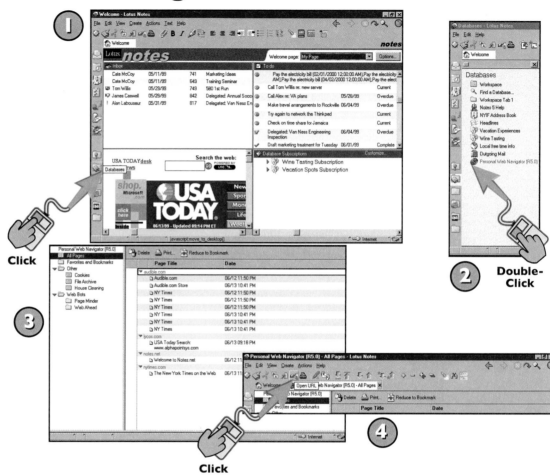

Start Here

Click

Double-Click

Click

✅ **Can't Find the Personal Web Navigator?**
The Personal Web Navigator is on the list of databases if you chose Notes as your default Internet browser in the Internet location document.

① Click the **Databases** bookmark to display a list of databases.

② Double-click **Personal Web Navigator (R5.0)** to open the Notes browser.

③ The left side of the Personal Web Navigator screen contains a list of categories. On the right is a list of stored pages along with the date and time they were visited.

④ Click the **Open URL** SmartIcon to display a typing area for a URL address.

Next Step

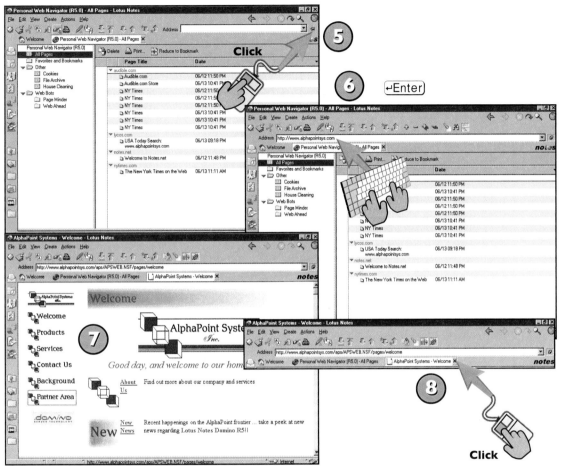

Browser Buttons
The **Go Back**, **Go Forward**, and **Stop** browser buttons are located in the top-right corner of the browser. Using **Go Back** and **Go Forward** does not close the window tab.

Collapsible Categories
Each Internet domain name you visit is added to the list of pages as a collapsible category. Within the category are the names of the individual pages visited at the site. Some pages don't have unique titles because of how the hosting site created the page.

5 Click the push pin to the right of the URL address typing area to pin it open permanently.

6 Type a URL into the typing area, and press the **Enter** key to retrieve the Web page.

7 The Web page is displayed.

8 Click the **Close (X)** button on the Web page's window tab to close the window.

Task 4: Bookmarking a Web Page

You can add a URL as a bookmark directly to your Notes client.

✓ **Renaming a Bookmark**
The full URL name is used as the bookmark title with a prefix of Personal Web Navigator. This could make the name too long to read easily on the bookmark; change it by right-clicking the bookmark and choosing **Rename**.

✓ **Bookmark Welcome Page**
You can use a bookmark to replace the Welcome page as the Notes starting point. With a bookmark selected, right-click and choose the **Set Bookmark as Home Page** option.

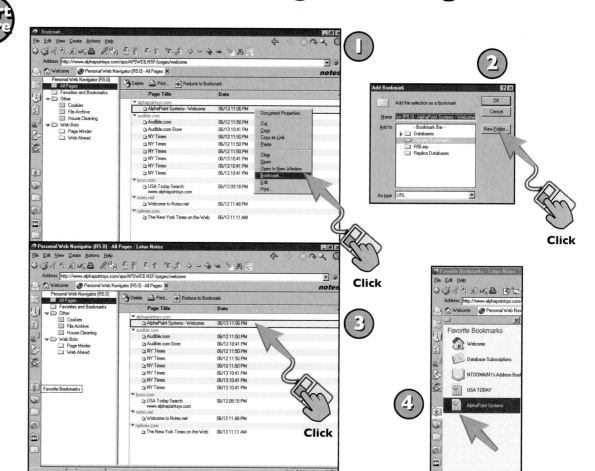

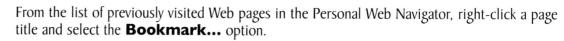

Start Here

Click

Click

Click

① From the list of previously visited Web pages in the Personal Web Navigator, right-click a page title and select the **Bookmark...** option.

② Choose an existing bookmark to add the URL to, or create a new folder for it by clicking the **New Folder** button. Click the **OK** button to add the bookmark.

③ Click the bookmark you selected in step 2.

④ The page is added.

End Task

Task 5: Enabling Background Agents for the Web

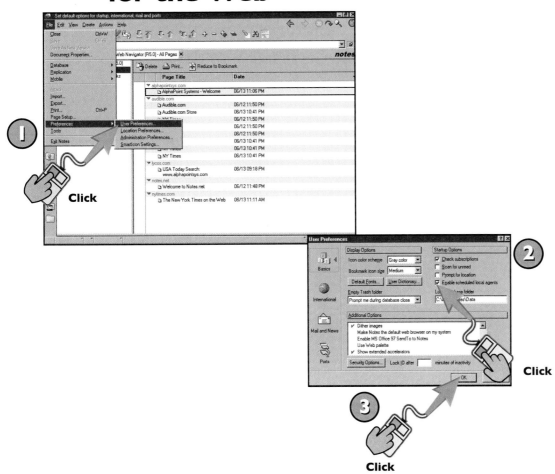

① Click

② Click

③ Click

The Notes browser has several background agents that can be used to automate Internet activities. *Agents* in Notes are preprogrammed utilities that help automate tasks. To use background agents, the Notes client needs to allow scheduled local agents to run. This is an option you configure in your Notes preferences.

① Choose **File**, **Preferences**, **User Preferences...**.

② Check the **Enable scheduled local agents** check box.

③ Click the **OK** button to save your changes.

✓ Background Agents
Web Ahead is a feature that automatically runs behind the scenes. This is called a *background agent* or a *scheduled local agent* in Notes.

Web Ahead is a Web automation feature, or *Web Bot*, in the Notes Personal Web Navigator. Before you go offline, you can use Web Ahead to retrieve up to four levels of links. The pages are then stored so that you can read them offline.

Task 6: Configuring Web Ahead for Offline Browsing

Start Here!

① Click

② Click

③ Click

① In the Personal Web Navigator, choose **Actions**, **Internet Options…**.

② Click the **Preload Web pages** drop-down arrow, and select the number of levels of pages Notes should retrieve.

③ Click the **Enable Web Ahead** button to activate this feature.

Next Step

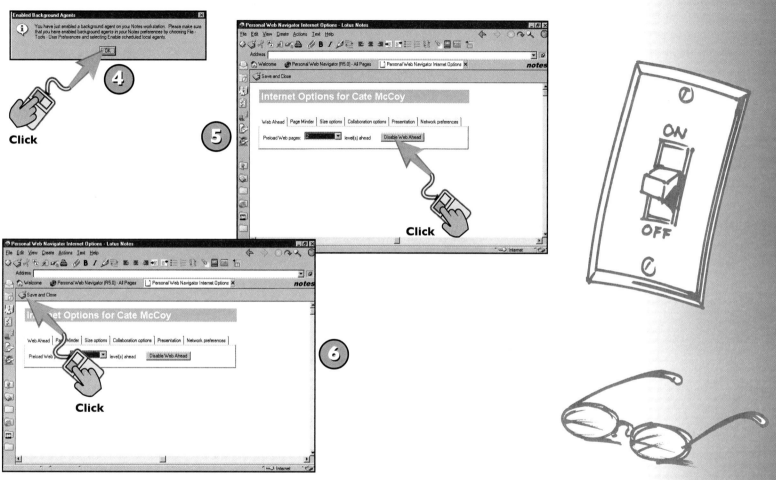

4 A warning message reminds you to enable background agents for your Notes client (refer to Task 5 in this section for instructions on doing this). Click the **OK** button.

5 Web Ahead is enabled. To disable this feature in the future, revisit this page (choose **Actions**, **Internet Options...**) and click the **Disable Web Ahead** button.

6 Click the **Save and Close** button to save your changes.

Task 7: Setting Up Page Minder for Automatic Updates

Page Minder is a Web automation feature, also called a *Web Bot,* which monitors pages for information that has changed. You specify the URL address to monitor, and when an update is detected, Notes sends you a summary notification message or mails you the actual page.

✓ **Send To**
The Send To area is small and shows only a portion of the complete Notes address of the person who will be notified by Page Minder.

✓ **Notifying a Group**
You can notify a group of Notes' users about updates to a page. Use the Address button to select a group from your Personal Name and Address Book.

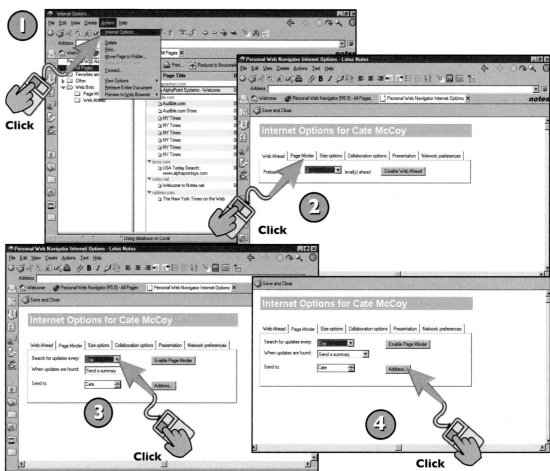

1. In the Personal Web Navigator, choose **Actions**, **Internet Options....**

2. Click the **Page Minder** tab.

3. Click the **Search for updates every** drop-down arrow and select Every hour, Every four hours, Once per day, or Once per week to specify how often Page Minder should check for updates.

4. By default, Page Minder notifies you about changes. To instruct Page Minder to notify a different person, click the **Address** button and choose the person you want.

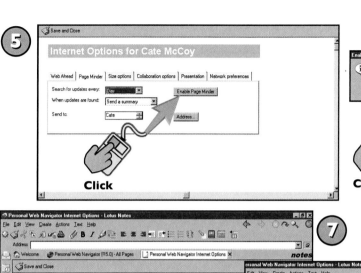

Click

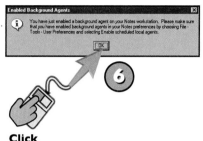

Click

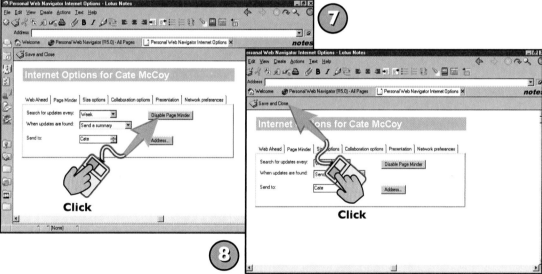

Click

Click

(5) Click the **Enable Page Minder** button to activate the Web Bot.

(6) A warning message displays, reminding you to enable local scheduled agents (refer to Task 5). Click **OK**.

(7) Page Minder is enabled. To disable this feature in the future, revisit this page (choose **Actions**, **Internet Options...**) and click the **Disable Page Minder** button.

(8) Click the **Save and Close** button to save your changes.

End Task

Task 8: Starting the Page Minder Web Bot

After setting up Page Minder with a monitor frequency and a person to notify, you need to start it on its way! To do this, visit the page you want to monitor and then add it to the Page Minder folder.

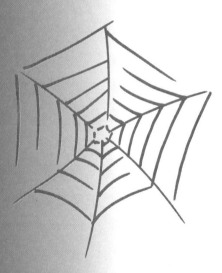

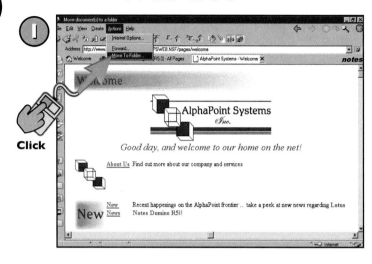

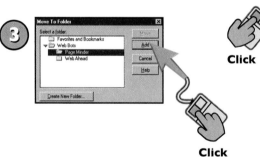

Start Here

Click

Click

Click

✓ **Drag and Drop**
You can bypass the Move to Folder window by dragging the Web page directly into the Page Minder folder in the Personal Web Navigator.

① With a Web page displayed in the Personal Web Navigator, choose **Actions**, **Move To Folder...**.

② Select the **Page Minder** folder.

③ Click the **Add** button.

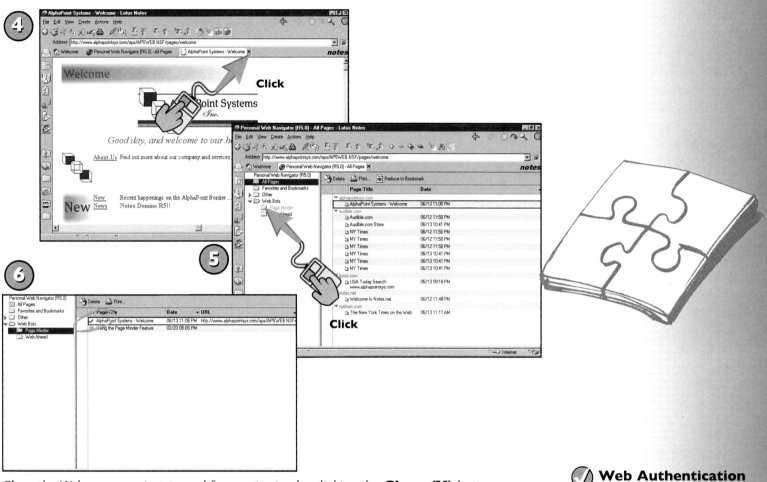

Click

Click

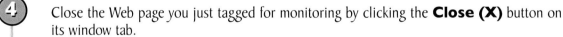

(4) Close the Web page you just tagged for monitoring by clicking the **Close (X)** button on its window tab.

(5) In the Personal Web Navigator, click the **Page Minder** folder to confirm that the Web Bot is active.

(6) A green check mark appears in the margin of active Page Minder documents.

✓ **Web Authentication**
If you're asked for a user ID and password to enter a page that you want to monitor, Notes saves the user ID and password you type and uses it each time Page Minder checks for updates.

End Task

Task 9: Creating Accounts for Internet Communication

You can configure Notes to check your Internet mail account—for instance, AOL. To do so, you create an account in your personal address book to allow Notes to communicate with the Internet using the Simple Mail Transfer Protocol (SMTP), the Post Office Protocol (POP), Internet News Transfer Protocol (NNTP), and the Lightweight Directory Protocol (LDAP). Don't worry about the big words and strange acronyms, this stuff is a snap to set up in Notes!

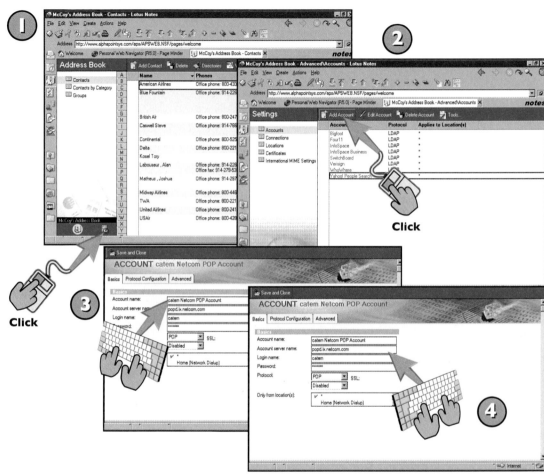

Click

Click

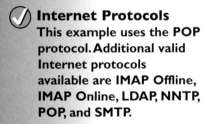

Internet Protocols
This example uses the **POP** protocol. Additional valid Internet protocols available are **IMAP Offline, IMAP Online, LDAP, NNTP, POP,** and **SMTP.**

① From inside your personal address book, click the **Advanced Settings** icon in the bottom-right corner of the Navigator pane.

② The list of accounts shows that several LDAP accounts were created for you by Notes. LDAP is used for searching the Internet for information. Click the **Add Account** button.

③ Type a descriptive name of your own choosing for the account.

④ Using information provided by your Internet provider, type the account server name, login name, and password.

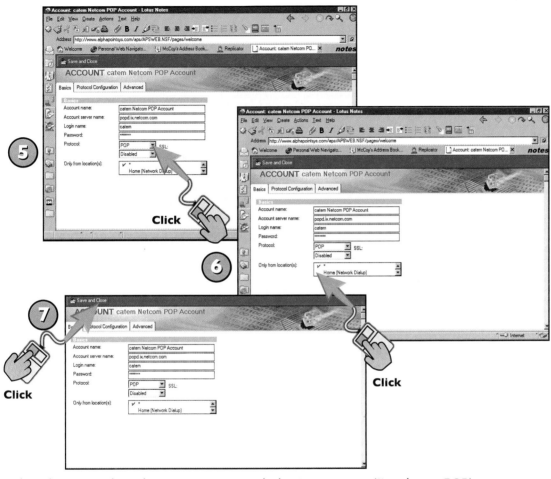

Click

Click

Click

5 Select the protocol used to communicate with this Internet site (I've chosen POP).

6 Select the location document(s) that can use this account.

7 Click the **Save and Close** button to save your settings.

Passwords
Your password is saved in Notes, but asterisks are used on screen to hide the information.

Location Documents
The asterisk means that all location documents can use this account.

Firewalls, Gateways, and Proxies
Organizations often put firewall, gateway, and proxy security in place to protect Domino servers from hackers. If this type of security is in place, check with your Domino System Administrator for instructions on how to access your Internet mail from a Lotus Notes client.

Which Protocol Should I Use?
Your Internet provider can tell you what kind of protocol to use with its service. In general, **SMTP** is used for sending Internet mail and **POP** is used to receive Internet mail.

End Task

After creating a location document that can access the Internet and configuring an account document with the specifics of your Internet account, you're ready to send and receive Internet mail!

✓ Mail File
Be sure that the location document you're using correctly identifies your mail filename. You can check it by clicking the location on the status bar—for example, Office—to display a list of all locations. Click **Edit Current** to open the location document and, on the Mail tab, verify that your Notes user ID name is listed in the mail file field.

✓ POP Account
You'll need to create a Post Office Protocol (POP) account to receive Internet mail. (POP is one of the choices you have when you create an Internet account.

Task 10: Sending and Receiving Internet Mail

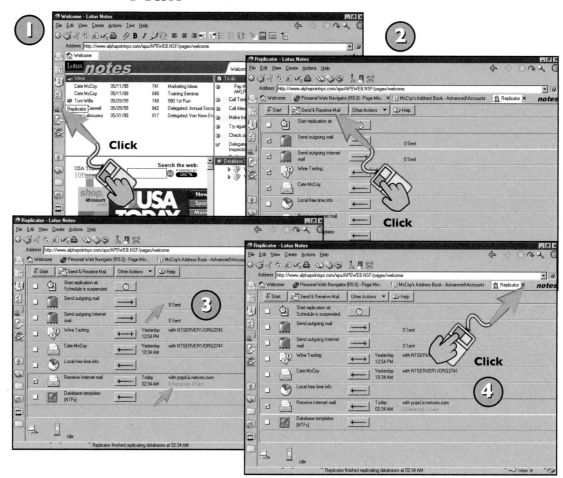

① Click the **Replicator** bookmark to open the Replicator page. (Notes uses the replication process to send and receive Internet mail.)

② Click the **Send & Receive Mail** button to initiate mail replication.

③ When the replication process is complete, mail has been sent and received. You'll see status messages next to the blue arrows notifying you of the number of received and sent messages.

④ Close the **Replicator** page by clicking the **Close (X)** button on its window tab.

Task 11: Reading Your Internet Mail

Start Here

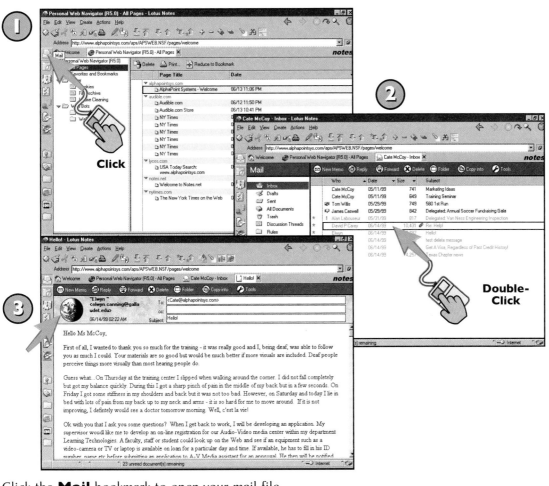

Internet mail is deposited in the mail file that you specified in the current location document. The process of reading Internet mail is the same as reading Notes mail.

① Click the **Mail** bookmark to open your mail file.

② The messages appear in your Inbox with unread marks in the margin. Double-click a message to open it.

③ The Internet email looks just like a Notes email, but its header includes a globe icon to signal that it was received from the Internet and your Internet mail address appears in the To: area.

✓ **Text Format**
The body of an Internet email displays text without any formatting such as bolding, italics, and color.

End Task

Task 12: Configuring Notes to Access NNTP Newsgroups

Internet newsgroups are similar to Lotus Notes discussion databases. People share questions, thoughts, and comments on a topic by subscribing to a central repository. You can set up a Notes account document to monitor an Internet newsgroup, receiving updates in your Inbox.

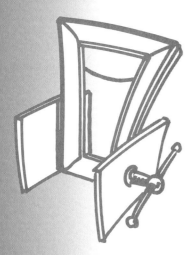

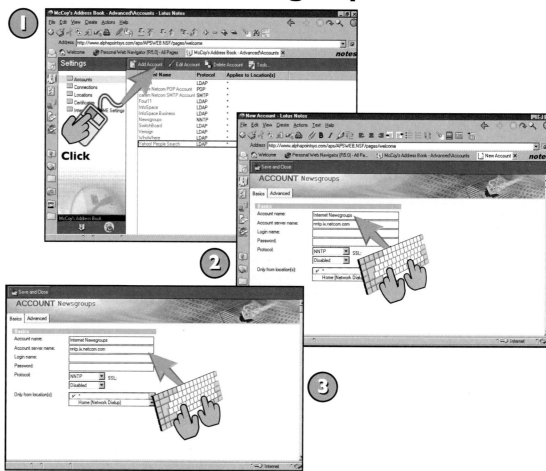

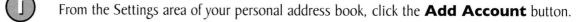

✓ **Newsgroup Address**
Most Internet service providers (ISPs) have their own address for newsgroups. Check their support page to find out what it is.

① From the Settings area of your personal address book, click the **Add Account** button.

② Type a name to describe the account. The name you type here will be used to create a new Notes database to store the Internet newsgroup headers.

③ Type the Internet address of the newsgroup. Many newsgroups are not open to the public, so you may see an error message.

Next Step

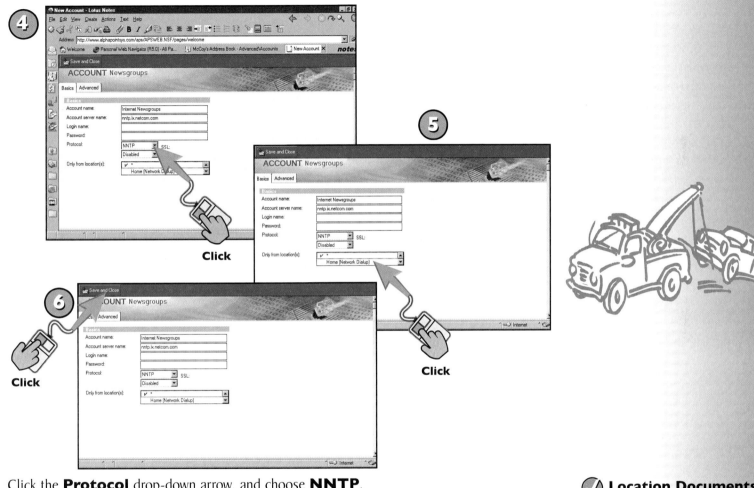

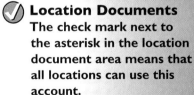

④ Click the **Protocol** drop-down arrow, and choose **NNTP**.

⑤ Select the location documents allowed to use this NNTP account.

⑥ Click the **Save and Close** button to save your changes.

Location Documents
The check mark next to the asterisk in the location document area means that all locations can use this account.

Task 13: Reading Newsgroup Messages

Notes stores messages from newsgroups in a database. The process of creating an account for a newsgroup also creates the database. To select a group within a newsgroup and then read the messages, you need to open the database.

✓ Loading Newsgroups
Before displaying the list of available groups within the newsgroup, Notes must retrieve the entire list from the remote server. This step takes a long time the first time you do it, and after that it goes faster because Notes looks only for incremental changes to the group list.

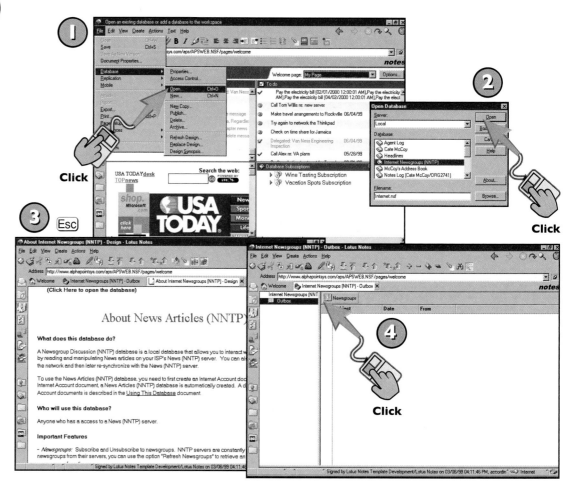

Start Here

Click

Click

Click

① Choose **File**, **Database**, **Open…**.

② Locate and select the newsgroup database (the account name you typed in step 2 of the preceding task is its title). Click the **Open** button.

③ When you open the newsgroup database for the first time, a screen of information text is displayed telling you about the database. Press the **Esc** key on the keyboard to close it.

④ Click the **Newsgroups** button to retrieve a list of groups that below to the newsgroup server you specified.

Next Step

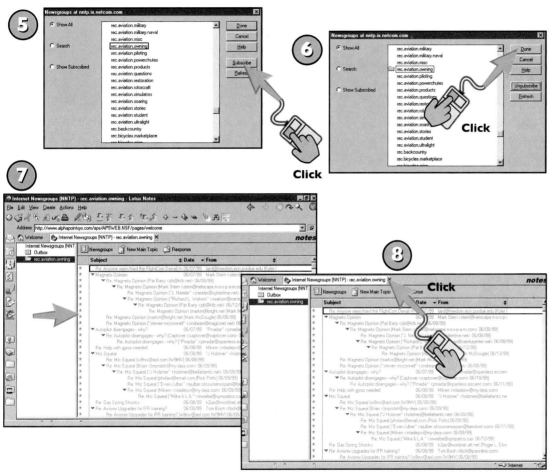

5 A list of all the newsgroups is displayed. Select one and click the **Subscribe** button.

6 Click the **Done** button to exit from the list of groups.

7 Notes retrieves the messages and then displays them in list form. You can read the messages just like you read a discussion group message.

8 Click the **Close (X)** button to exit from the newsgroup database.

✅ **Incremental Updates**
When you click the newsgroup, all new messages since the last time you checked are downloaded from the newsgroup server.

✅ **Bookmark the Newsgroup**
An entry for the newsgroup database was automatically added to the Databases bookmark.

End Task

Find Information— Anywhere!

Few things are as frustrating as knowing that a piece of information exists somewhere within your reach, but not knowing exactly where it is. The Notes R5 search engine has been tuned to help you quickly find electronic information by looking in a wide variety of places. Typing in a word is the starting point in Notes to find just about anything whether it's a Notes database, a piece of information within a database, or data on the Web. In this section, we'll explore the many powerful search options in R5.

Tasks

Task 1: Locating a Database

Databases are used as containers to store information in Lotus Notes, so finding a database is the starting point to working with the information. Each Notes server keeps a catalog of database titles on that server, which is itself a database (no surprise there!). A database search looks through this catalog of database titles.

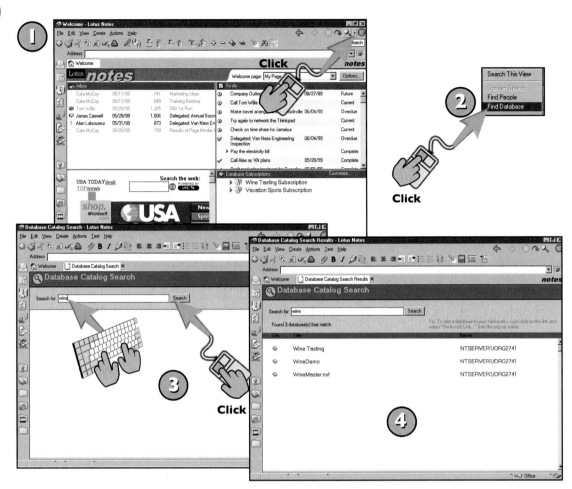

 Welcome Page
Searching for a database can be done directly from the Welcome page by searching the Notes Database catalog.

 Bookmark a Database
You can bookmark a database found in the search by right-clicking the title of a database and choosing the **Bookmark Link** option.

 Click the drop-down arrow to the right of the **Search** button (the button with the magnifying glass on it).

 Select the **Find Database** option to open a typing area.

 Type a keyword that might appear in the database title, and click the **Search** button to start the search process.

4 A list of databases that contains the keyword is displayed.

Task 2: Jumping to a Document in a View

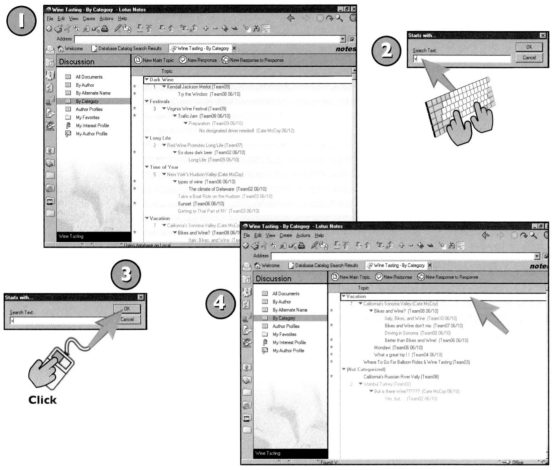

A *view* is a list of documents in a database. Often, the list of documents is longer than what can fit on one screen. If the first column of information is sorted, you can jump to a document by typing in a few of the starting letters in the first column. For instance, if the first column contains last names sorted alphabetically, typing the letters Mc jumps you from the currently selected document to ones with last names starting with "Mc."

Click

✅ **Where to Type**
The act of starting to type activates a search that does a letter by letter match on the first column of data. You don't need to have the mouse pointer in a typing area.

✅ **How Much to Type?**
In a long list, type the maximum number of characters that you're sure of for an initial match, and then use the scrollbar to move to the exact document.

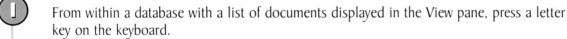

1. From within a database with a list of documents displayed in the View pane, press a letter key on the keyboard.

2. Type as much of the word as you can in the **Starts with**… search box that appears.

3. Click **OK** to start the search.

4. The black rectangle signals that a selected category or document matches the letter(s) you typed.

Task 3: Finding and Replacing Data

You can search for a word or phrase within an open document. If the document is in edit mode, the **Replace** option is available, and can be used to replace one word or phrase for another. The **Replace and Find Next** button is grayed out unless the document is in edit mode.

 Search Menu
The drop-down arrow for the **Search** button defaults to finding text in the current document, so clicking directly on the **Search** button does exactly this.

 The Edit Menu
The **Edit** menu on the main menu bar contains **Find/Replace** and **Find Next** options, which also displays this search window.

 Keyboard Shortcuts
Ctrl+G is the shortcut key to open the **Find** search window, while **Ctrl+F** opens the **Find/Replace** window in edit mode.

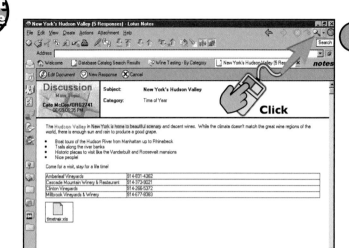

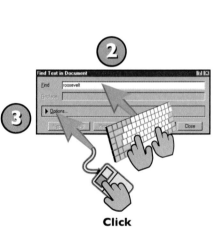

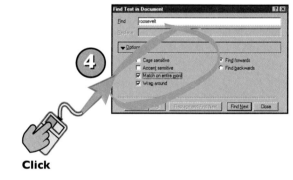

From within a document, click the **Search** button.

The **Find Text in Document** dialog box appears. Type a word or phrase in the **Find** area.

Click **Options** to expand the dialog box and display additional search options.

Choose one or all of the check boxes for case-sensitive, accent-sensitive, match on entire word, and wrap-around searches.

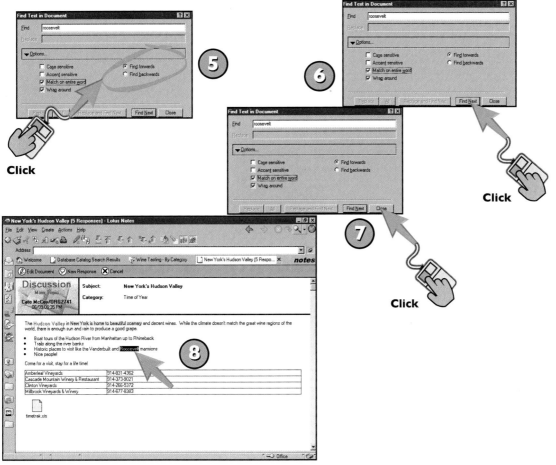

⑤ Click the **Find forwards** (searches from the current position of your mouse position to the end of the document) or **Find backwards** (searches from the current position to the end of the document) option button.

⑥ Click the **Find Next** button to start the search.

⑦ Click the **Close** button to remove the search dialog box, because it can obscure information on the screen.

⑧ With the search window closed, the search word you entered in step 2 is visible, highlighted in black.

Task 4: Displaying and Using the Search Bar

Views contain many documents. If you don't know which document contains the information you need, you can search for it. Notes has a very flexible search engine built into it that searches for words and phrases within documents that are part of the current view. This is known as *full-text searching*.

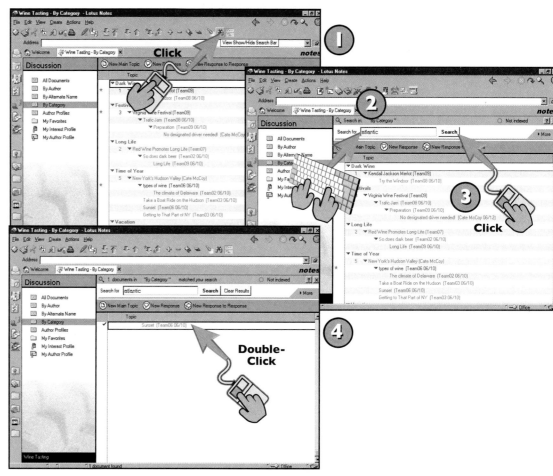

✅ **The View Menu**
You can open the search bar by choosing **View, Search Bar.**

✅ **Enter Key**
After you type a word or phrase in the **Search for** field, press the **Enter** key on the keyboard to start the search.

① Click the **View Show/Hide Search Bar** SmartIcon.

② Type a word or phrase in the **Search for** field.

③ Click the **Search** button to look for documents that contain the search word or phrase you typed in step 2.

④ The documents that contain the word or phrase are listed. Double-click a document to open it, and you'll see the search word or phrase.

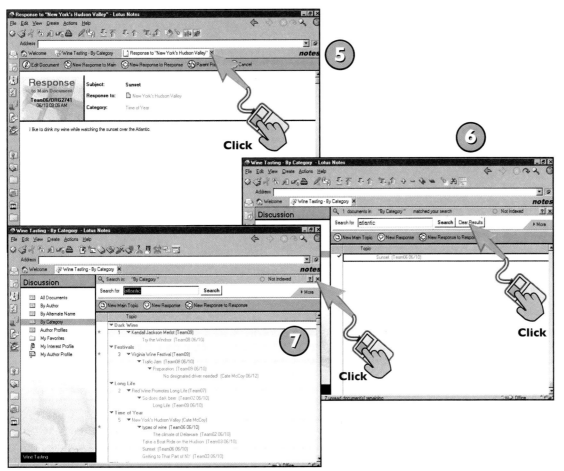

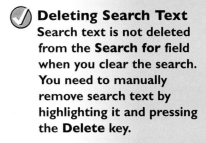

(5) Close the document by clicking the **Close (X)** button on its window tab.

(6) Click the **Clear Results** button to restore the view that was originally searched.

(7) Click the **Close (X)** button on the **Search** window to exit the search facility.

✓ **Deleting Search Text**
Search text is not deleted from the **Search for** field when you clear the search. You need to manually remove search text by highlighting it and pressing the **Delete** key.

Task 5: Saving a Search Query

After you've built a search query that returns the documents you need, you can save the query and reuse it later. This saves you from having to think through the logic or remember keywords. The search criteria are saved with a name you provide; you will use this name to run the search later.

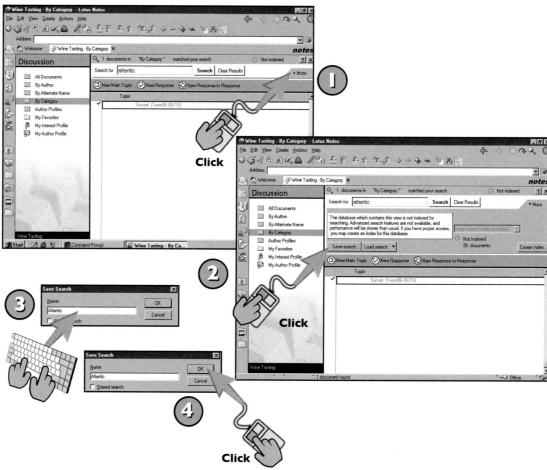

Start Here

Click

Click

Click

1 With the search results displayed from a full-text search, click the **More** option.

2 Click the **Save search...** button.

3 Type a name for the search results, perhaps using the word or part of the phrase used to conduct the search. You'll use this name to retrieve the results in the future.

4 Click **OK** to save the search with the name you typed.

Next Step

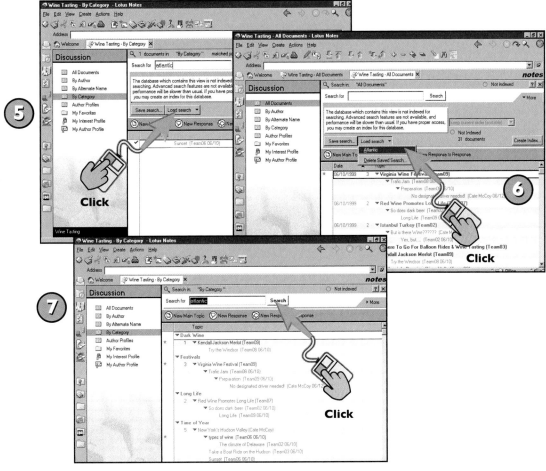

5   To retrieve a saved search query, click the **Load search** button.

6   Click the name of the search you want to retrieve.

7   Your search query is placed in the search box, highlighted in black. Click the **Search** button to run the search; the search results appear onscreen.

End Task

Task 6: Indexing a Database

When you do a full-text search of a view to find words in a document, Notes looks through every document looking for a match to your search criteria. This process can be slow if there are many documents. One way to improve the speed of the search is to add an index to the database that is used in full-text searches.

✓ **Rights to Create an Index**

You can create an index on any database that is stored on your own PC, like a replica copy of your mail file database or the Help database. Your system administrator can index databases stored on a server.

✓ **Full-Text Index Options**

Each of the options (indexing attached files, encrypted fields, sentence breaks, and case-sensitivity) will make your searches better but will also use more disk space on your PC.

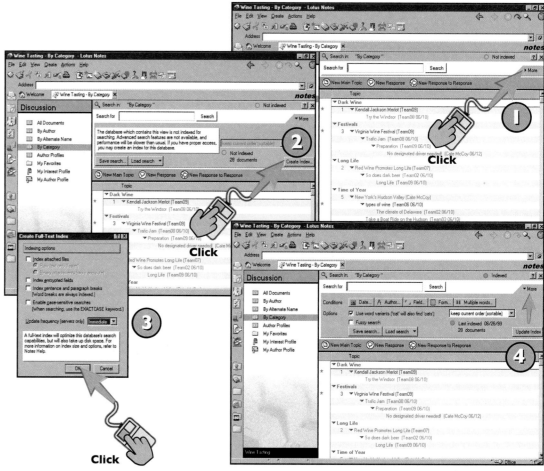

① From the search bar, click the **More** option.

② The phrase Not Indexed and the presence of the Create Index button indicate that the database does not yet have an index. Click the **Create Index...** button.

③ The check box options let you fine-tune the way the index is created. Select what you need, and click **OK** to create the index.

④ When the index is created, an **Update Index** button and information on when the index was last updated appear in the **More** area of the search bar.

Task 7: Using Conditions in a Full-Text Index Search

Start Here

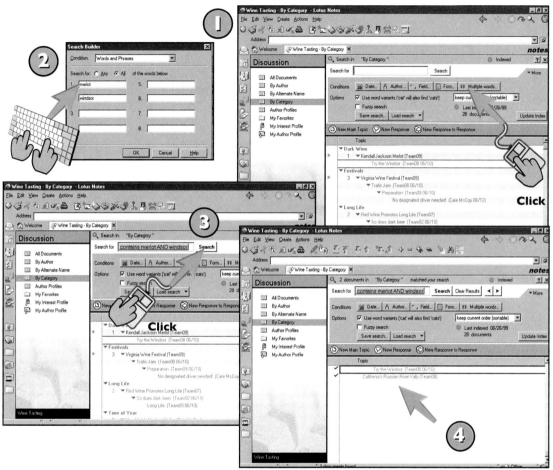

After a database has an index, you can use complex conditions to fine-tune your search. Buttons are provided to do searches for documents that are specific to a particular date, author, field value, database form, or that contain a combination of words or phrases. Multiple-word searches find documents that contain combinations of words.

✓ Phrases

In Notes, *phrases* are groups of words that appear next to one another. For instance, "Saturday night" is a phrase. Documents that meet the criteria would need these words to appear side by side in exactly this order.

✓ Any or All

The **Any** option finds any documents that contain any of the words that you specify. The **All** option finds only those documents that contain all the words you specify. The default is **Any**.

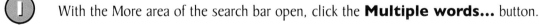

1 With the More area of the search bar open, click the **Multiple words...** button.

2 Type up to eight words to search for—in this case, because the **All** option button is selected, the search returns documents that contain both **merlot** and **windsor**—and click **OK**.

3 Click the **Search** button.

4 A list of documents that contain the words or phrases specified is returned.

Task 8: Working with Full-Text Index Search Options

Does searching for a word cause you difficulty because you're not sure of the spelling? Do you want to search for both the singular and plural versions of a word? Either way, Notes can help. The word variant and fuzzy search capabilities of Notes lets you type as much as you know, and Notes returns matches that are either exact or close to what you typed depending on the options you choose.

Start Here

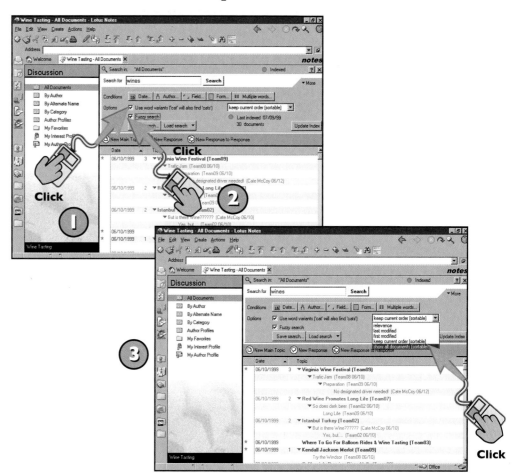

Click

Click

Click

Click

✓ **Word Variants**
In this example, the search word is **wines**, so only exact matches on this word will be found. A variant of this would have included the singular expression wine as well.

✓ **Fuzzy Searches**
When the **Fuzzy** option is marked, Notes finds words that are similar to what you typed but not exact. This flexible option allows for misspelled words as well as word phrases.

In the search area with the **More** options displayed, click the **Use word variants** check box to perform an inexact search (this returns words like *wine* and *winery* in addition to the search word, *wines*).

2 Click the **Fuzzy search** check box if you want words and phrases that are similar to the search word to be returned by the search.

3 Click the drop-down arrow to tailor how the results are displayed (see the tip "Result Order" for more information).

Next Step

 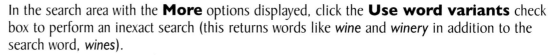

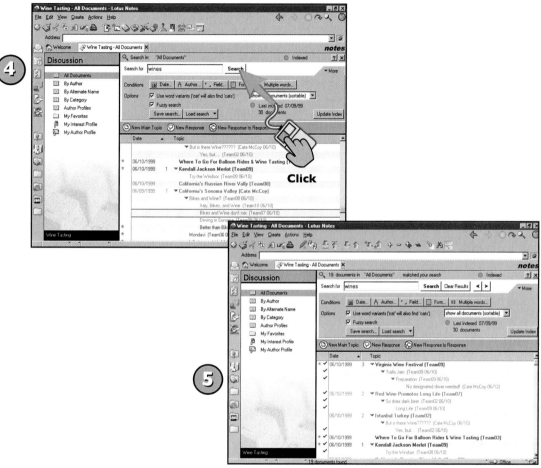

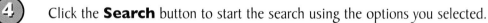
(4) Click the **Search** button to start the search using the options you selected.

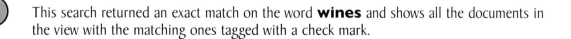
(5) This search returned an exact match on the word **wines** and shows all the documents in the view with the matching ones tagged with a check mark.

Result Order

By default, documents that result from a search are displayed in the order they are found. This may be alphabetical, by date, or by physical storage. For more control over the sort order, use the drop-down arrow to sort by relevance to the number of times the search words are found or the date the documents were modified. You can also choose to display all documents in the database with ones matching the criteria tagged with a check mark.

The R5 client puts the Internet on the Lotus Notes desktop. If you have a live Internet connection, you can search Internet directories for a person's email address without leaving Notes. An Internet directory is similar to a phone book, however, it lists people and their Internet email addresses instead of their phone numbers.

✅ **LDAP**

LDAP is an acronym that stands for Lightweight Directory Access Protocol. A directory that is LDAP-enabled makes its information accessible for searching.

✅ **Details Button**

Additional information beyond the name and email address may be available depending on the information provided by the user when he created the account. Click the **Details** button to view any public information available for the selected account.

Task 9: Searching Internet Directories from Notes

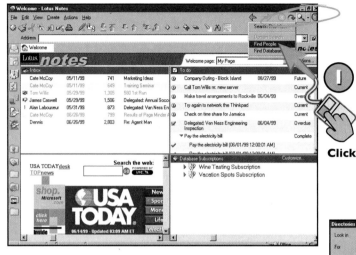

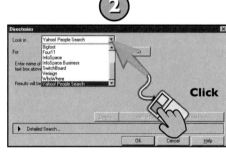

Click

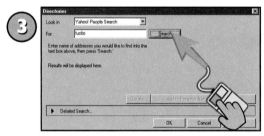

Click

Click

1. Click the drop-down arrow next to the **Search** button, and select the **Find People** option.

2. Click the **Look in** drop-down arrow and select one of the listed directories to search for a person's email address.

3. Type the last name of the person you want to find in the directory you selected, and click the **Search** button.

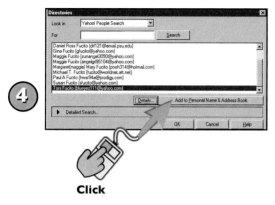

Click

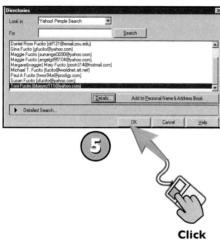

Click

The search results are displayed in the Directories window. Select a name from the list and click the **Add to Personal Name & Address Book** button to save the selected address in your personal directory.

Click **OK** to close the Directories window.

Task 10: Refining an Internet Person Search

You can set search criteria to help you find a person using an Internet directory. The Detailed Search area of the Directories search window helps you build search criteria that can contain multiple search conditions.

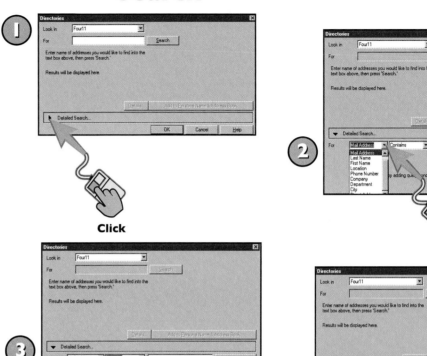

Click

Click

Click

Start Here

✓ **Opening the Directories Dialog Box**
Refer to step 1 of the preceding task if you need help opening the Directories dialog box.

✓ **Search Operations**
Seven search operations are found in the drop-down list in step 2. Select **Is** to perform an exact match, or **Isn't** to exclude the text you enter from the search. **Begins With** and **Ends With** perform a match on as many letters as you type, and **Sounds Like** uses the phonetic alphabet to search for audio-type matches.

 In the Directories dialog box, select a directory to look in (refer to step 2 of the preceding task if you need help with this), and click the **Detailed Search...** option on the bottom part of the screen.

 Click the first drop-down arrow to select what you want to search for; in this example, the option to search the Internet mail address is selected.

 Click the second drop-down arrow to choose the kind of match you want to make.

 Type the word you want to search for in the field on the right.

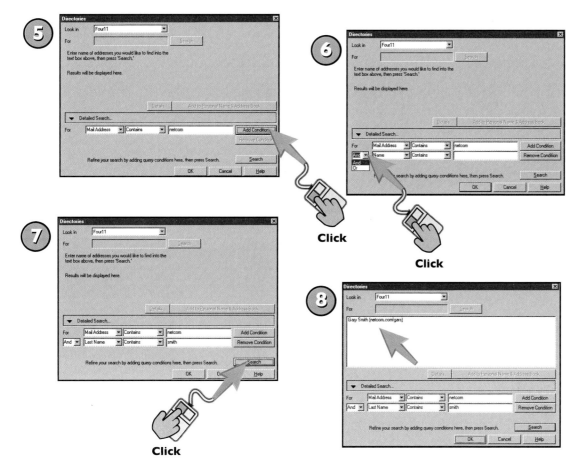

Click

Click

Click

(5) In the case of this search, the FourII directory is searched for Internet mail addresses that contain the word **netcom**. Click **Add Condition** to continue refining the search criteria.

(6) Click the first drop-down arrow on the new row to specify how this row works in relation to the criteria specified in the previous row (the options are **And** and **Or**).

(7) Repeat steps 2, 3, and 4 (but this time in the new row) to specify a second set of match criteria, and click the **Search** button.

(8) The search results are displayed.

✓ **And**
The **And** option returns results that include people that meet the criteria in the previous row as well as the criteria in the new row.

✓ **Or**
The **Or** option returns results that satisfy at least one of the row's search criteria.

End Task

Essential Security Concepts

Lotus Notes R5 has several security features that help protect your information from the malicious intent of others. At the heart of Notes security is your user ID and password. In this section, you'll learn how to manage and use your user ID from a security perspective.

Tasks

Task 1: Locking Your Notes Client Automatically

Believe it or not, the biggest security risk to your stored data is you! Whenever you leave your PC unattended and logged in to Lotus Notes, your information is at risk. To help protect your information, you can quickly log out of Notes or have Notes lock your machine automatically for you after a period of inactivity.

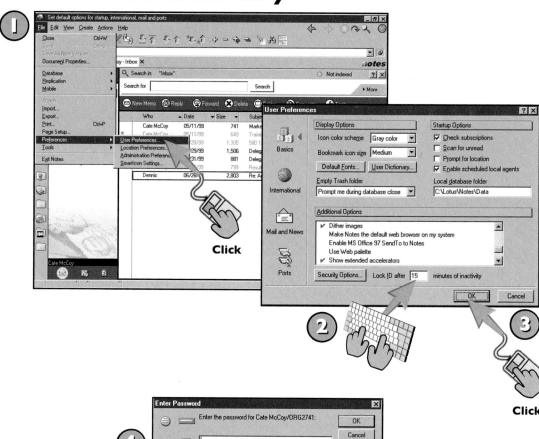

Click

Click

Enter Password

Enter the password for Cate McCoy/ORG2741:

OK

Cancel

✓ **Manual Locking**
You can manually lock Notes (log out) at any time by pressing the **F5** key on the keyboard. The menu command will also lock your Notes session.

(1) Choose **File**, **Preferences**, **User Preferences...**.

(2) In the Lock ID after field, type the number of minutes Notes should wait during a period of inactivity before locking your Notes client.

(3) Click the **OK** button to save your change.

(4) The next time you try to use Notes after it has been idle for the number of minutes you specified in step 2, you'll be prompted for your password.

Task 2: Sharing Your PC with Other Users

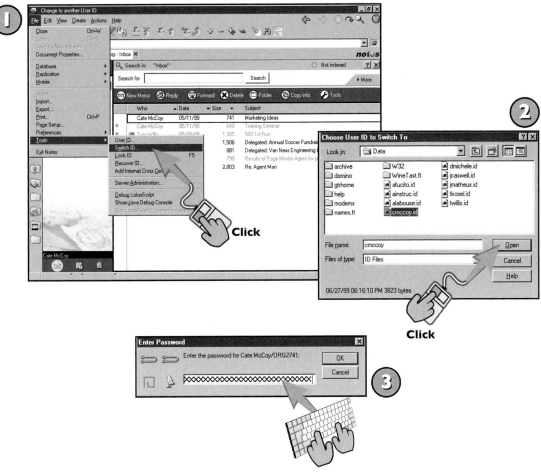

Click

Click

Your Notes user ID is unique to you. If you share a PC with someone else, that person should have his or her own Notes ID. You can switch between user IDs so that each person's information is kept private.

① Choose **File**, **Tools**, **Switch ID...**. The current user is logged out of Notes, closing all open databases.

② A dialog box enabling you to choose a different user ID opens. Navigate to and select a file with an **.id** extension, and then click the **Open** button to switch to that ID.

③ You are prompted for the password for that ID. Type the correct password to log in under the new ID.

✓ **Welcome Page**
The information about what is stored on your personal Welcome page is not stored with your ID file. When you use your ID at another person's PC, that person's Welcome page is displayed. Choose File, Database, Open to access your databases.

Task 3: Changing Your User ID Password

You can think of your user ID as the front door to your Lotus Notes desktop. That makes the password the key that opens the door, and you should keep it safe. One of the easiest ways to protect your ID is to change your password frequently.

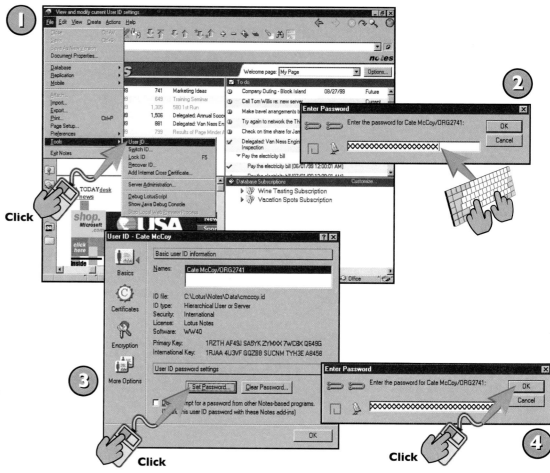

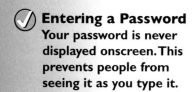

✓ **Entering a Password**
Your password is never displayed onscreen. This prevents people from seeing it as you type it.

1. Choose **File**, **Tools**, **User ID...**.

2. You're immediately prompted for your current password; type it and click the **OK** button.

3. Click the **Set Password...** button.

4. You're asked for your current password again (this is to make sure you actually have permission to change it). Type it, and click **OK**.

Next Step

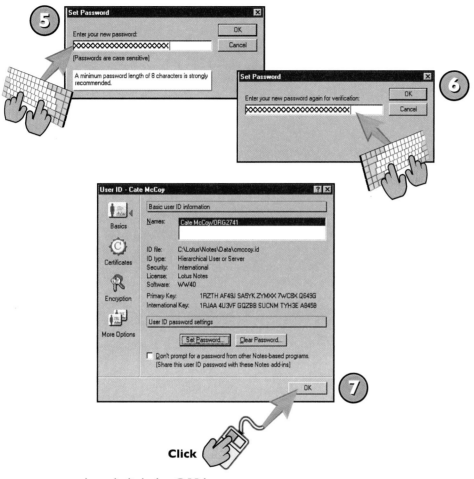

Click

(5) Type a new password, and click the **OK** button.

(6) Type your new password again (to make sure you typed it correctly the first time), and click **OK**.

(7) Your password has been changed. Click **OK** to close the User ID screen.

End Task

If you forget your password, lose your user ID file, or the ID file becomes corrupted, you can recover the ID with the help of your Domino System Administrator. Your Administrator will give you a temporary recovery password. You'll need to visit the Administrator in person to get the password, however, because you won't have email until you can get back into Notes!

✅ **Recovery ID Dialog Box**

You may have to click the **Cancel** button several times before the Choose ID File to Recover window is displayed.

✅ **Number of Authorized Administrators**

Your organization may require more than one Administrator to provide you with recovery passwords. If so, obtain a recovery password from each administrator, and enter each password you receive one at a time.

Task 4: Recovering from a Forgotten Password

Click

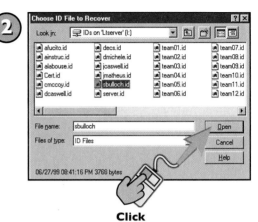

Click

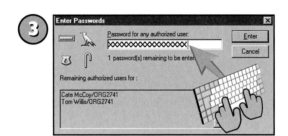

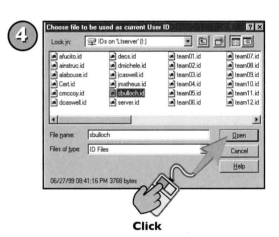

Click

① When you attempt to open Lotus Notes, click the **Cancel** button to close the password request window.

② A dialog box opens that allows you to choose an ID file to recover; in this example, several users have IDs on this workstation. Select your ID, and click the **Open** button.

③ Type the password the System Administrator provided to you, and click the **Enter** button.

④ Choose your user ID from the list, and click the **Open** button.

Next Step

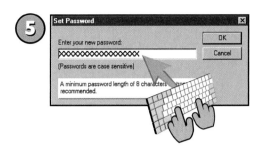

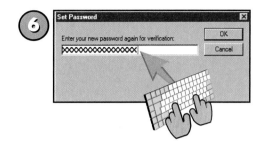

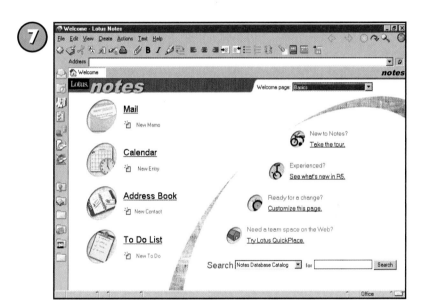

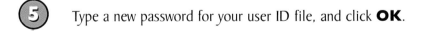

5 Type a new password for your user ID file, and click **OK**.

6 Type your new password again to confirm it, and click the **OK** button.

7 Your Lotus Notes desktop is displayed.

Task 5: Working with Certificates

Certificates in Notes are like visas to enter other countries. A certificate gives you permission to access a server. The server might be a Domino server, or it may be a non-Domino server on the Internet that you need to access. Certificates are stored in your user ID file, and like visas, they expire on a specified date and need to be renewed. You can view and manage your certificates in the User ID dialog box.

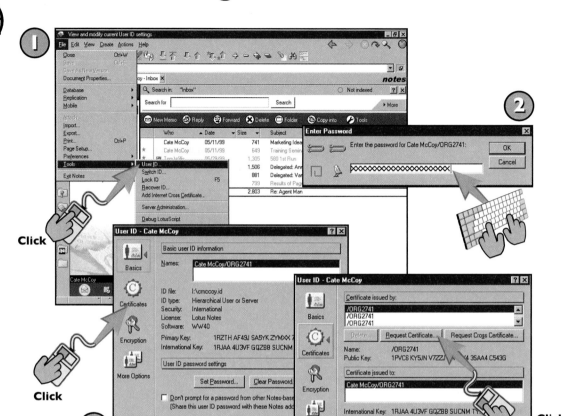

(✓) **Types of Certificates**
Notes has two kinds of certificates: those that work on Domino networks and those that work on the Internet. Internet certificates are also known as *X.509 certificates.*

(1) Choose **File**, **Tools**, **User ID...**.

(2) Type your password and click **OK**.

(3) Click the **Certificates** icon.

(4) The list of existing certificates is displayed as well as the name of the certifier (the organization granting permission). To request a new certificate, click the **Request Certificate...** button.

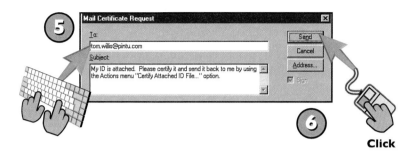

Click

Click

(5) Type the email address of the person from whom you're requesting a certificate. This person is known as the certification administrator.

(6) Click the **Send** button to email the certificate request.

(7) Click the **OK** button to close the User ID window. You'll be notified by email of the success or failure of your request to the remote server for a certificate.

Certificate or Cross Certificate?

For an individual and a server to communicate, they must be able to authenticate; meaning that they need a certificate in common. If they don't descend from a common ancestor, both the server and the individual need to exchange cross certificates.

Requesting a Cross Certificate

Requesting a cross certificate works in the same way as a regular certificate request except that your ID file is automatically attached to your email request.

Finding the Email Address You Need

You might get the email address of the certification administrator from whom you're requesting a certificate from your System Administrator or from the Internet, on a public Web page describing the remote server's information.

End Task

Task 6: Encrypting Mail Messages

Encryption is the process of scrambling data so that it can't be easily read. An encryption key is a piece of information used to scramble or unscramble the information. Two encryption keys (built-in to your user ID file) work in tandem to protect your information: a public key and a private key. You can apply them to any or all the mail messages you create.

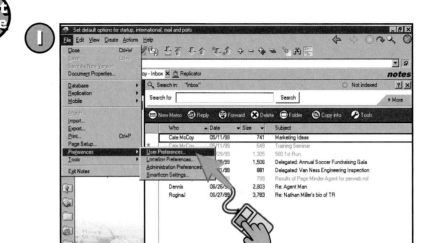

Click

Click

 Public Key
Your *public* key is used to send and encrypt information.

 Private Key
Your *private* key is used to receive and decrypt information.

Choose **File**, **Preferences**, **User Preferences…**.

Click the **Mail and News** icon.

Next Step

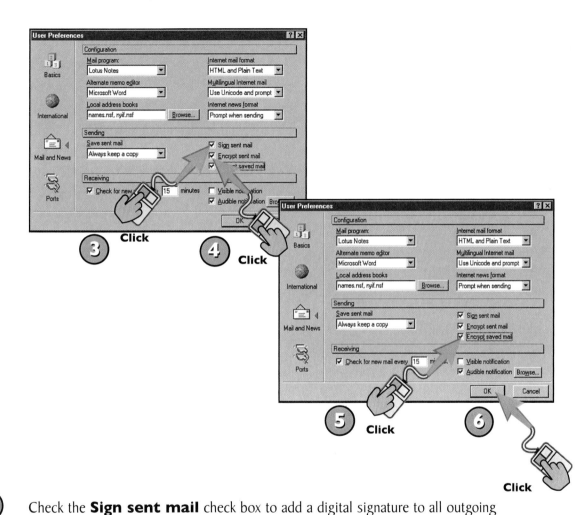

Click ③

Click ④

Click ⑤

Click ⑥

③ Check the **Sign sent mail** check box to add a digital signature to all outgoing messages.

④ Check the **Encrypt sent mail** check box to scramble all outgoing messages.

⑤ Check the **Encrypt saved mail** check box to scramble any incoming messages that you save. (Note: any mail received prior to turning on this option is not encrypted.)

⑥ Click **OK** to save your changes.

✅ **Digital Signatures**
Digital signatures guarantee that your electronic message is not tampered with between the time that you send it and when the recipient receives it. Also, signatures guarantee that the person who sent the message is really who they say they are.

End Task

Task 7: Overriding Encryption Settings

Each new email you create gives you the opportunity to change the encryption settings for the memo. If you've turned encryption on system-wide, you can turn it off for the memo you're writing. Likewise, if you haven't enabled system-wide encryption, you can encrypt an individual mail memo.

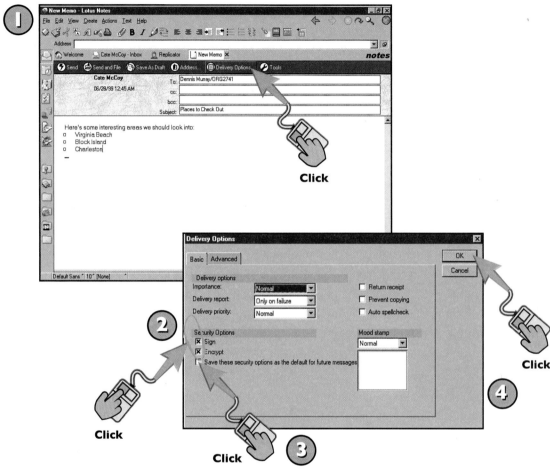

Click

Click

Click

Click

✓ **System Settings**
The security options show what is currently in effect for all messages. Here, signing and encrypting is enabled for all messages.

1. From within an email you're writing, click the **Delivery Options** button.

2. To override the system settings for this email, click the **Sign** or the **Encrypt** options.

3. You can make the settings of this email the system-wide settings by checking the **Save these security options as the default for future messages** check box.

4. Click the **OK** button to save your changes.

Task 8: Receiving a Mailed Encryption Key

Start Here

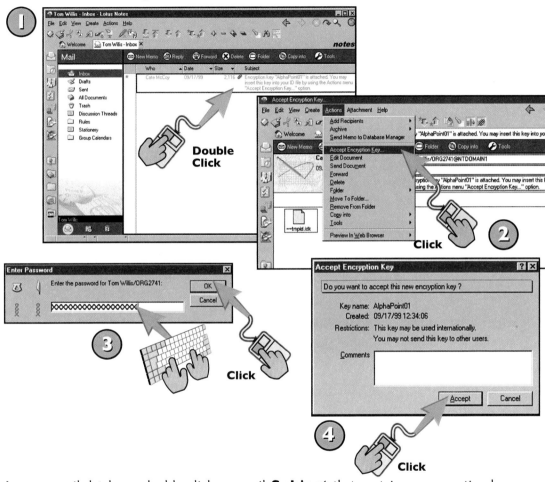

Double Click

Click

②

Click

③

Click

④

Click

Some database applications contain documents that have encrypted fields of data. The encrypted data can only be viewed if you have a key that will decrypt it. The key is supplied by the designer of the database. One of the ways you might receive this key is as an email.

①　In your email database, double-click an email **Subject** that contains an encryption key as an attachment.

②　From the menu of the opened email, select **Actions**, then **Accept Encryption Key...** to receive the key.

③　You'll be prompted to enter your password at this point because the key is password-protected. Type your password and click **OK**.

④　To accept the encryption key and automatically insert it into your ID file, click the **Accept** button. You can add a comment to describe the key if you like.

End Task

Task 9: Importing an Encryption Key from a File

An encryption key may be supplied to you in an external file, perhaps on a disk. Importing a key allows you to use the key.

Start Here

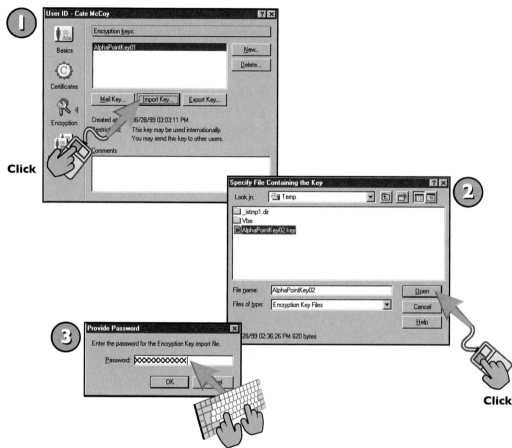

Click

Click

1 From within the Encryption area of the User ID screen, select a key and click the **Import Key...** button.

2 Navigate to the directory where you stored the key file sent to you by the person who sent you the encrypted document, select it from the list, and click the **Open** button.

3 If the key was password-protected when it was created, you're prompted to enter that password (get this information from the person who sent you the file). Type the password and click **OK**.

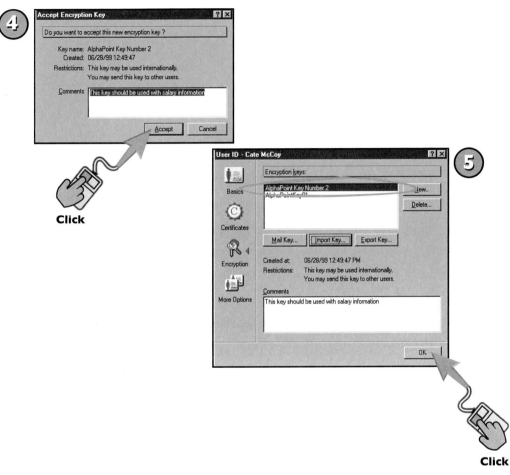

Click

Click

(4) Confirm that you want to accept the encryption key by clicking the **Accept** button.

(5) The imported key is added to the list of existing keys. Click **OK** to close the User ID window.

Key Comment
When you import a key, you can type your own comment to describe the key in the Accept Encryption Key dialog box.

Task 10: Encrypting a Document

Documents can contain fields of encrypted information that can't be viewed without an encryption key. For documents you create with fields that you want to encrypt, you need to apply an existing encryption key to the document.

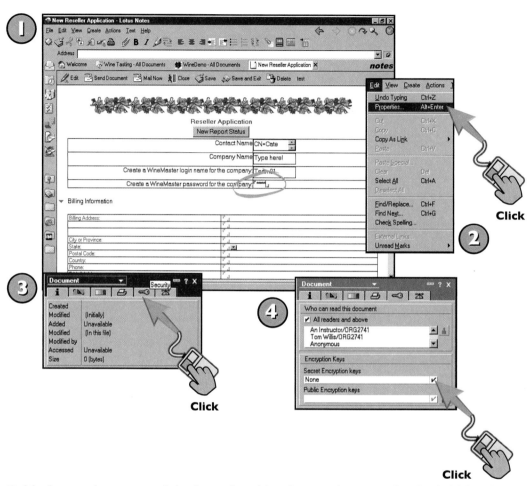

Click

Click

Click

✓ **Encryptable Fields**
The designer of a database determines if a field can be encrypted.

✓ **Properties Drop-Down List**
If the title bar for the properties doesn't say Document, click the drop-down arrow and click the Document option.

Fields that can be encrypted display with red borders. In this example, the field for the WineMaster company password can be encrypted.

To encrypt the field, apply an encryption key to it by choosing **Edit**, **Properties...**.

Click the **Security** tab.

Click the check mark in the **Secret Encryption keys** area.

Next Step

Click

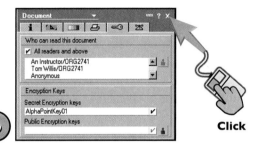

Click

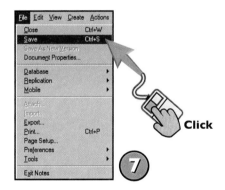

Click

(5) Click the name of one of the encryption key names listed to select it as the key to use for this document. The field will be encrypted using this key when the document is saved.

(6) The key name you selected is displayed in the dialog box. Close the dialog box by clicking the **Close (X)** button.

(7) Choose **File**, **Save** to save the document. This applies the encryption key you chose to the field that has been enabled for encryption.

✓ **Encrypted Fields**
Fields that have been encrypted do not display in the document when someone without the key opens it. Only unencrypted fields are visible.

Glossary

A

action bar   A horizontal area at the top of a database with buttons that perform tasks specific to the application; for instance, Send is an action button in the mail file database that sends an email. This is also referred to as the *button bar*.

address book   A Lotus Notes database that contains the names and email addresses of Notes users and other people with which you interact. You have a personal address book for your own use. There is also an address book on each Notes Domino server that contains the email addresses of people in your organization.

agents   Automated activities in a database; for example, the out-of-office email agent notifies people when you are out of the office.

alarm   A sound you can trigger to activate for calendar events.

archiving   Copying data out of the current database to a separate database.

attachment   A file that is stored as part of a Notes document, for example, a photograph or Microsoft Word document. It can be viewed, launched, or detached. Emails you receive and create can contain attachments.

B

authenticate   The process where Notes challenges you to supply a password as you access a database or other restricted-use resources.

BCC   Blind courtesy copy. A copy of an email you write is sent to another user at the same time it is sent to the original recipient, but without the information being visible to the original recipient.

bookmark   Links located along the left vertical border of the Notes client; a bookmark can be a folder that contains database bookmark icons.

button bar   See *action bar*.

C

calendar   A specially formatted view that displays dates and times of appointments, anniversaries, events, and meetings.

CC   Courtesy copy. Sends a copy of an email you write to another user at the same time it is sent to the original recipient. Courtesy copy information is visible to the original recipient.

certificates   Certificates grant permission to access a remote server until the certificate expires.

client   A piece of software or hardware connected to a server for the purpose of sharing information. A Notes client is a software client. A software client is installed on a hardware client like a PC.

connection document   A document you can create and access through the Advanced icon of your personal address book that tells Notes how to connect to a remote resource—for instance, dialing into a Notes server using a modem.

context-sensitive help   Online help that's available by pressing the FI key on the keyboard; the help is specific to the current task being performed.

D

database   A container for related information—for instance, an address book. All documents, views, and folders in Notes are stored in databases.

detach   The process used to copy the contents of a file attached to a Notes document to the hard drive of a computer.

directory   A list of email usernames and addresses. The Notes Domino directory contains information about all users on the server.

document   A record of information in a Notes database (like an email memo) that contains fields of data.

drafts   An email that you create but do not send; it is saved in a Draft system folder and can be finished and sent at any time.

E

electronic signature   A digital identifier added to an email that guarantees that the information was not tampered with during transmission from the originator to the recipient, and that the originator is the author of the message.

encryption key   A unique identifier that is generated by Lotus Notes and given a name you choose. The key is applied to mail and fields of data as a locking mechanism. Two types of encryption keys are stored in your Notes user ID: a public key for sending and encrypting information and a private key for receiving and decrypting information.

F

field   A piece of information contained in a document.

full-text index   A set of internal computer directions that helps Notes quickly find information that you search for in a Notes database. Each database can have a full-text index.

G–H

group   A set of people to whom email and calendar entries can refer as a unit. Personal groups are created in your personal address book; a server's address book is controlled by the System Administrator and also contains groups.

group calendars   Calendars that can track the availability of several people at one time.

I–K

ISP   Internet service provider. A company that provides Web services and access to the Internet through a phone number.

keyboard shortcut   A set of keys on the keyboard that, when pressed at the same time, simulate options available on the menu bar. The Alt, Ctrl, and Shift keys are often used in combination with other keys (for example, Ctrl+F).

L

LAN   Local area network. Servers and clients connected to one another via cables to share information, files, and printers.

LDAP   Lightweight Directory Access Protocol. A special way to format address information in a directory (like an address book) that is used on the Internet.

letterhead   A graphic that can be added to the top of all emails you send.

location document   A document you can create and access through the Advanced icon of your personal address book that tells Notes where you are when you're using Notes—for instance, on a network or using a phone connection.

M

mail rules   Special filters you create to help automatically manage and process email.

modem   A piece of equipment attached externally or internally to a computer to allow it to talk to other computers using an ordinary phone line.

N–O

navigator buttons   Buttons at the top-right corner of the Notes client that provide fast access to searches, the Internet, and moving forward and backward through information displayed in pages on the screen.

Notes Minder   A utility facility that monitors your Notes mail file database without having Lotus Notes running.

P–Q

Page Minder   A feature of the Notes Personal Web Navigator that monitors specific Web pages for updates and notifies you with an informational email.

pane   An area on the Lotus Notes desktop that displays information—for example, the View pane and the Navigator pane.

password   A special security device that you use to access information in a Notes database when challenged during the authentication process.

permanent pen   A setting that allows you to control the default font, color, and size for text you are typing.

R

replica database   A database that is connected to another database and shares contents. At certain points in time, the databases are synchronized (replicated) and information is exchanged and duplicated between the databases.

replicate   The process of exchanging information between replica copies of databases so that each is synchronized to the other.

replicator   An area in Notes that lists, and can be used to manage, the replication process.

replicator bookmark   A bookmark link available along the left border of the Notes client that provides access to the list of replica databases currently available.

S

server   A piece of software or hardware connected to clients for the purpose of sharing information. A Notes Domino server is software installed on high-powered hardware.

signatures   Text information or graphics you can add to the end of memos you create.

SmartIcons   Single-click buttons that provide fast access to commands also available from the menu, usually with more clicks of the mouse required.

stationery   A standard email that can be used over and over again; similar to a form letter.

subscriptions   Subscriptions enable you to receive updates in your email as they are added to Notes discussion databases.

T–V

To Do list   A set of documents that contain activities you track for progress and completion; to do tasks are added to your personal calendar.

user ID   A file that contains your Notes username, your password, your public and private encryption keys, and your certificates to use other servers.

W–Z

Web Ahead   A feature of the Notes Personal Web Navigator that automatically gathers several levels of Web links when a page is accessed so that the information can be read offline at a later time.

Web bot   Refers to automated routines that handle tasks and run on Web-like robots.

Welcome page   The customizable launch point in the Notes client; it is the first area you see when you open the Notes client.

window tab   Rectangular areas that appear above a document and below the menu and SmartIcons and that contain a Close (×) button. You can have many window tabs open at one time.

A

B

C

D

K

L

M

N

T

The IT site you asked for...

InformIT is a complete online library delivering information, technology, reference, training, news and opinion to IT professionals, students and corporate users.

Find IT Solutions Here!

www.informit.com